PRAISE FOR *P*
BRANDS

For anyone considering a career in sustainability, ESG communications or purpose, or those who are already well on their way in the industry, Sandy Skees' new book absolutely required reading. Easy to read, pragmatic and actionable, it's a must.
Susan McPherson, CEO, McPherson Strategies

I've long been a fan of Sandy Skees. Her intelligence, humanity and sense of purpose encourages those around her to be better in every way. Now, that same thoughtful encouragement is available in *Purposeful Brands*, a must-read for anyone connected to organizations and brands that want to do good and show up sincerely as allies, advocates and activists. I can think of no one better than Sandy to learn from on this topic. This is the book brand communicators need right now.
Soon Mee Kim, Chief Diversity, Equity & Inclusion Officer, Omnicom Communications Consultancy Network

I've known Sandy for nearly a decade through both our professional networks & affiliations and by engaging Sandy as ESG counsel for large purpose-driven campaigns throughout my career. Sandy has expertise driving progress across key environmental and social issues, but what makes her unique is her equally skilled ability in communications and stakeholder engagement. Even as our industry continues to grow, Sandy's voice remains a strong and influential one. She has always pushed leaders in the space to think without limits – which is critically needed to achieve progress – whether we're tackling climate change or driving DEI&B. She is also always part of the solution through her own leadership or by making valuable connections. Sandy's knowledge on the issues clearly comes through in *Purposeful Brands* but what makes this book so valuable and different from others in the genre is that in addition to helping make the business case, Sandy offers actionable steps that can be taken to advance your brand on its ESG journey. The book is engaging, easy to read and provides a true masterclass on building the purpose-driven brand of the future. I highly recommend it!
Joanne Dwyer, VP, Corporate Social Responsibility, PetSmart

Business today has changed forever and every leader must urgently rise to the challenge of answering *how* we build a regenerative and equitable world. Sandy Skees leverages her deep expertise to deliver a doers guide for tomorrow's world that cuts through the complexity and makes it possible for your business to thrive and better our future.

Simon Mainwaring, bestselling author of *We First* and *Lead With We*

Purposeful Brands

How Purpose and Sustainability Drive
Brand Value and Positive Change

Sandy Skees

KoganPage

Publisher's note

Every possible effort has been made to ensure that the information contained in this book is accurate at the time of going to press, and the publishers and authors cannot accept responsibility for any errors or omissions, however caused. No responsibility for loss or damage occasioned to any person acting, or refraining from action, as a result of the material in this publication can be accepted by the editor, the publisher or the author.

First published in Great Britain and the United States in 2023 by Kogan Page Limited

2nd Floor, 45 Gee Street
London
EC1V 3RS
United Kingdom

8 W 38th Street, Suite 902
New York, NY 10018
USA

4737/23 Ansari Road
Daryaganj
New Delhi 110002
India

www.koganpage.com

Kogan Page books are printed on paper from sustainable forests.

ISBNs

Hardback   978 1 3986 0985 3
Paperback   978 1 3986 0983 9
Ebook   978 1 3986 0984 6

British Library Cataloguing-in-Publication Data

A CIP record for this book is available from the British Library.

Library of Congress Control Number
2023933905

Typeset by Integra Software Services, Pondicherry
Print production managed by Jellyfish
Printed and bound by CPI Group (UK) Ltd, Croydon, CR0 4YY

To my wife Mary, who always sees what's possible.

To Christina, Elisabeth, and Mike, whose future deserves a thriving planet and an equitable society.

To all generations to come—we did not accept the status quo.

CONTENTS

LIST OF FIGURES AND TABLES

Figures

Tables

ACKNOWLEDGMENTS

Writing a book is harder than I thought it would be, but the process itself was also invigorating and clarifying. A "Yes—and" experience through and through. This process has given me the chance to look back over my career and refine decades of work into an approach and methodology to share with the wider world. Together, I hope we will create a regenerative planet and the equitable society we all want.

First, I am deeply grateful for my wife Mary and our family— Christina, Elisabeth, and Mike—you are why I do the work I do. To my large extended families of three generations, may we all continue to see the world as a place where hope and progress are realized. And to all my pals—you know who you are—you keep me inspired, fed, restored, moving, and laughing through this life.

I am grateful for the community of courageous optimists who have been on the purpose and sustainability journey with me. I want to thank Laura Lee Alben who was the catalyst to helping me find work worth doing. To Irene Tsouprake who shares a "Yes—and" life. To Annie Longsworth whose friendship has gifted me with wit and wisdom for more than a decade. To collaborators and friends whose advice and work have helped shape this book: Pamela Gil-Alabaster, Paula Alexander, Virgine Helias, Lisa Kenney, Maddy Kulkarni, Mark Lee, Renee Lertzman, PhD, KoAnn Vikoren Skrzyniarz, and Andrew Winston.

To my Porter Novelli colleagues whose smarts, creativity, and collaborative spirit have been just the right alchemy to design and deliver real purpose work together: Conroy Boxhill, Kristin Fontanilla, Gina Lindblad, Erin Osher, and Cali Pitchell. Finally, to Lisa Unsworth whose talent has expanded my thinking and helped shape many purposeful brands.

Lastly, to all of you who are now part of the community of change agents—welcome to a lifelong journey of seeing the world with optimism tempered by the reality of challenges and entrenched worldviews. It's whole-hearted work and I am glad to be linking arms with all of you.

ABOUT THE AUTHOR

Sandra Skees believes there is power in leveraging purpose as a platform to help companies, their employees, customers, and investors create a regenerative and equitable world. For over 30 years, she has worked with global brands, start-ups, and scale-up companies to align their purpose, sustainability and environment, social, governance (ESG), and diversity, equity, inclusion (DEI) with compelling communications. She leads the global purpose and impact group for Porter Novelli, a strategic communications company. Over the years, her work with corporations, nonprofits, and non-governmental organizations has been focused on climate and environmental issues, LGBTQ+ and racial equity, recycling and waste, renewable energy, supply chain, and human rights issues. She sits on numerous boards and is a seasoned speaker on brand, messaging, and sustainability strategy.

CONTRIBUTORS

Christina Deogracias (image design)
Pamela Gil-Alabaster
Paula Alexander
Virgine Helias
Lisa Kenney
Maddy Kulkarni
Renee Lertzman, PhD
Annie Longsworth
KoAnn Vikoren Skrzyniarz
Andrew Winston

Introduction
Purpose, Sustainability and ESG Work Together

In 2007, I hit a wall. For more than twenty years I had built a successful career as a communicator. From marketing to brand building, public relations, and corporate communications, I had two decades of experience helping companies—and a handful of nonprofits—articulate their mission and vision. My degree in sociology gave me a grounding in how to interrogate what groups believe or why they behave the way they do. I grew to appreciate how human action and consciousness both shape and are shaped by surrounding cultural and social structures. In my communications career, I honed my storytelling ability, understanding that, in the end, we absorb information using both our left and right brains, by activating our head and our heart. That for persuasion and connection to be effective, they require authenticity and emotion.

I'd spent years honing my craft in developing just the right message to persuade people to buy computers and printers, phones, and barbeque sauce. Even select the perfect casket for their loved one. All in service to essentially one thing: increase revenue to drive up the stock price. Which is an important and valued ambition for any business. And yet... by 2007, I knew that I could not launch one more product or vapid marketing campaign. I knew I needed to use my storytelling skills for some greater good.

Just as I was contemplating a career move that might have included law school, or med school, a friend sent me an email promoting a new conference, Sustainable Brands. Touting speakers from Aveda, the Gap, and Walmart, the first-of-its-kind business-to-business (B2B) conference promised to focus "on helping the mainstream business community learn from the leaders how to build and communicate about their sustainable brands. To provide a place for leaders from corporations and their PR, advertising, creative consultants and agencies to come together to talk about the issues, challenges and best practices surrounding building and communicating their company's environmental and social value propositions."

Attending that inaugural conference changed my career trajectory and, for the first time, showed me that not only could communications be in service to a greater purpose, but that business itself could be organized to solve environmental and social challenges. It was the beginning of both my personal and professional purpose journey.

So, I left my big job at a large global communications agency to start my own sustainability firm. I asked myself: did I want to wake people up? Or did I want to work with those already awake? I decided to work with those who saw what I saw almost two decades ago—that respecting the planet and building an equitable society through commerce is full of possibilities for innovation, creativity, and success.

This book is the culmination of my years as a sustainability consultant and a strategic communicator helping big brands and start-ups, scale up companies and non-governmental organizations (NGOs) refine and articulate their purpose and explore how value creation can—and must—include responsibility to the commons. These are the shared resources that none of us own, but we all depend upon—air, water, ecosystems, habitats, and social systems like education, healthcare, and the arts.

What has begun to seem like common sense, or at least a shared viewpoint—that we need a thriving planet and a working society within which to operate a profitable business—was not always the case.

Businesses are grappling with pressure to define their company's purpose and provide a roadmap for its cascading implementation implications. Finding and defining purpose is just the beginning. A brand's purpose must be simple yet inspiring, authentic, and specific, all while differentiating a company's brand value. When done right, a crystalized purpose can drive innovation, employee engagement, customer loyalty, efficiencies, and resiliency against shifting cultural landscapes and emerging stakeholder power.

Purpose, sustainability, and environment, social, governance (ESG) are closely related but very different terms used for the way in which a company manages its footprint in the world. Think of ESG as process, policies, and rigorous reports. Sustainability is aspiration, vision, and strategy. All ladder up to purpose.

Essentially, sustainability is the strategy for operationalizing purpose through a rigorous ESG program.

From climate to diversity, from packaging and waste to labor and human rights, companies have a far-reaching set of activities that can have either positive or negative outcomes on the planet and society. A robust sustainability strategy and comprehensive ESG program have now been proven to be a consistent predictor of a well-run company. These are ones that carefully manage resources, reduce expensive waste, have minimal staff churn thanks to talent management and DEI programs that create a welcoming culture, and have the expansive policies, commitments, and organizational structure in place to ensure consistency in delivering strong ESG results.

Communication is an integral and often overlooked component in sustainability and ESG. Think about it this way. Businesses are used to providing ongoing communications across owned, earned, and paid channels when it comes to business updates, product marketing, brand advertising. I call this the language of business. A language that is expanding to now include the environmental and social footprint of companies as well.

This book is for chief communications officers (CCOs), chief marketing officers (CMOs), chief executive officers (CEOs), marketing directors, heads of marketing, marketing managers, brand strategists, brand consultants, PR and communications professionals, and agency leads on both the agency and client side.

Let's explore how purposeful brands find, operationalize, and communicate who they are and the change they want to create in the world through every aspect of their business.

Defining Your Brand's Purpose

01

Brand Purpose as Your North Star

In January of 2019, BlackRock chief Larry Fink told CEOs that fixing the planet and society's problems— in an increasingly divided world— was now their responsibility (Sorkin and de la Merced, 2019). At the time, BlackRock was the world's largest asset manager, with over $6 trillion in assets under management. Each year Fink issues a letter to the CEOs of its invested companies and in 2019 Fink's admonition for change was stark and pointed. He was clear that the purpose of a corporation was no longer to single-mindedly deliver shareholder value. Rather, he articulated a growing belief that the entire range of business assets and operations should be aimed at a greater good. He called this purpose. Purpose beyond profit. So began the stakeholder era.

He articulated what had become an increasingly strong imperative for business leaders. Many major investors had been urging executives to articulate a role for their companies beyond profit making, implying that doing so will positively affect their valuation. An excerpt from Fink's letter shows how his reframe of a corporation's responsibility and the benefits a commitment to purpose would yield began a sea change in how business value is now articulated and understood:

> Companies that fulfill their purpose and responsibilities to stakeholders reap rewards over the long-term. Companies that ignore them stumble and fail. This dynamic is becoming increasingly apparent as the public holds companies to more exacting standards. And it will continue to accelerate as Millennials—who today represent 35 percent of the workforce—express new expectations of the companies they work for, buy from, and invest in.
>
> (BlackRock, 2019)

I had been working in the sustainability and purpose sector for the previous eleven years and, with that one letter, the landscape of my work irrevocably changed.

What had been relegated to siloed corporate social responsibility (CSR) or corporate citizenship departments became of interest to the financial departments and investment community. As the leading voice for the investment community, Fink articulated the correlation between what he called purpose and two dimensions worth exploring further: risk and opportunity. Essentially, he understood that corporations were dependent on and beholden to a wide range of stakeholders. Something that seems apparent now but was a stark departure from decades of business thinking and scholarship.

Pre-Purpose

In September of 1970, the economist Milton Friedman published a *New York Times* article, "The social responsibility of business is to increase its profits." The core concept, detailed in its conclusion, became an unchallenged maxim in business and academia that: "there is one and only one social responsibility of business—to use its resources and engage in activities designed to increase its profits so long as it stays within the rules of the game, which is to say, engages in open and free competition without deception or fraud." For more than 50 years, businesses have fallen back on this economic theory as rationale for avoiding accepting the realities of externalities and the true power that a wide range of stakeholders have on the success of any business.

Externalities are the cumulative effect from the consumption, production, and investment decisions of individuals, households, and brands which often affect people not directly involved in those transactions. When the effects accumulate and begin touching society or the environment, they become the main reasons governments intervene in the economic sphere.

The most common example of a negative externality is pollution. In this case, a manufacturer makes decisions about materials and processes based only on the direct cost of and profit opportunity from production of a product. The decisions do not consider the indirect costs to those harmed by any resulting air or water pollution. The indirect costs include decreased quality of life, for example the case of a home owner near a smokestack; higher healthcare costs; or, when pollution harms activities such as tourism. Since the indirect costs are not borne by the manufacturer, and not passed on to the end user, the social or total costs of production are larger than the assumed costs, since these externalities are never accounted for in total production cost.

But that is changing. When I consult with clients, I usually start with the question, "Does the world need what you're making?" And then I ask them to consider how they make it, what it's made with, who makes it, and where. Each of these questions begins to get at the heart of a brand's purpose exploration.

But let's take a look at the other external forces that are pushing on companies to look at how their operational decisions (what they *do*) impacts the overall corporate story (what they *say*) and creates opportunities for greenwashing and green hushing—more on that later.

Silent Spring and the Environmental Protection Agency

In 1962, Rachel Carson published *Silent Spring*, which quickly became a bestseller. It used an accessible literary style rather than scientific jargon to present complicated data about what could happen to the natural and human world if the use of pesticides and chemicals went unchecked and unregulated. Much of the data was known by scientists but had not made its way to the general public or to governing bodies whose regulatory intervention would be needed if her concerns had any chance of being taken seriously. Carson argued that these chemicals not only killed bugs but also made their way up the food chain to threaten bird and fish populations and could eventually sicken children.

Not quite a year after *Silent Spring* was published, Carson testified before a Senate subcommittee on pesticides. She argued against the then-popular practice of indiscriminately spraying dichlorodiphenyltrichloroethane (DDT) across communities and farms to control mosquitoes and fire ants. By 1970, President Richard Nixon had signed the Environmental Protection Act which created the Environmental Protection Agency (EPA) and in 1982 the United States banned the domestic sale of DDT, except where public health concerns warranted its use. And while there have been challenges to her thesis and how she presented data, from my perspective what she illuminated was the reality of externalities. Her book used effective storytelling to show us how decisions made to solve one problem can create others.

Addressing unintended consequences is now part of a systems thinking approach that brands can address through purpose and sustainability.

The Birth of Purpose

From the 1970s through to 2019 there were what Mark Lee, Director at the SustainAbility Institute by ERM, calls waves of sustainability. In 2008, one year after my epiphany at the first Sustainable Brands conference, I saw Mark give a talk on the main stage that has stayed with me since. He described what he saw as the four waves of evolved environmentalism which had become known as sustainability. In 2008, Mark posited that we were entering the fourth wave. But he began his talk taking us through the waves, beginning with Rachel Carson and the formation of the EPA. This governmental regulatory foundation gave rise to the second wave in the mid-1980s and the early formation of green markets. These new companies and products were detailed in the book *The Green Consumer Guide* by John Elkington and Anita Roddick, the Body Shop's late founder and CEO. In many ways, this second wave is the heart of the sustainability movement because we could see the emergence of a new segment of buyers—people who were beginning to make product choices based on what impact the making or using of that product had on humans, other species, or the planet.

Wave three, which began in the late 1990s, saw the rise of NGO integration into the conversation. United Nations Chair Kofi Annan proposed the UN Global Compact, a precursor to the UN Sustainable

Development Goals which have been a guiding instrument for setting sustainability goals in the last decade. In 2008, Mark was predicting that as we entered the 2010s we faced real uncertainty about if a next wave of innovation and progress was coming. At that time, we had created a system of actors that included government regulation, an emerging "green" business sector, and a wide array of nonprofits, activists, and NGOs all looking at how to turn the vast array of business assets toward addressing some of the world's most compelling challenges.

This proved to be the fertile ground for purpose as a business driver.

The Business Roundtable

Following Larry Fink's letter in January of 2019, purpose became the latest business buzzword. Even now, more than a decade later, its meaning is still confused with mission, sustainability, and ESG— more about that later in this chapter. But let's take a closer look at how other organizations adopted the call for business purpose and responded to a shifting understanding of the role that business, capitalism, and markets have in the world.

By August of 2019, the United States Business Roundtable (BR) issued its guidance on the purpose of a corporation:

> Since 1978, Business Roundtable has periodically issued Principles of Corporate Governance. Each version of the document issued since 1997 has endorsed principles of shareholder primacy—that corporations exist principally to serve shareholders. With today's announcement, the new Statement supersedes previous statements and outlines a modern standard for corporate responsibility... While each of our individual companies serves its own corporate purpose, we share a fundamental commitment to all of our stakeholders.
> (Business Roundtable, 2019).

This new statement of purpose was signed by 181 US companies, many multinationals whose operational footprint spanned the globe. At that time, there was some widespread skepticism that any real change would come from such a commitment and two years later, a study by Harvard concluded that companies had largely not lived up to their purpose promise. "Our findings support the view that the BRT Statement did not represent a meaningful commitment," write the researchers, Lucian A Bebchuk and Roberto Tallarita of the Harvard Law School's Program on Corporate Governance. Instead, they say, the statement was "mostly for show" (Bebchuk and Tallarita, 2020).

The challenge of "stakeholderism," as Bebchuk and Tallarita explain, is that, as presented in the BR signed agreement, this commitment lacked governance rigor. Their paper analyzed the board commitments and structure of the signatory companies to determine whether any operational or governance changes had been made to accommodate the implications of such commitments as enumerated in the Business Roundtable's 2019 promise:

- Delivering value to our customers. We will further the tradition of American companies leading the way in meeting or exceeding customer expectations.

- Investing in our employees. This starts with compensating them fairly and providing important benefits. It also includes supporting them through training and education that help develop new skills for a rapidly changing world. We foster diversity and inclusion, dignity and respect.

- Dealing fairly and ethically with our suppliers. We are dedicated to serving as good partners to the other companies, large and small, that help us meet our missions.

- Supporting the communities in which we work. We respect the people in our communities and protect the environment by embracing sustainable practices across our businesses.

- Generating long-term value for shareholders, who provide the capital that allows companies to invest, grow, and innovate. We are committed to transparency and effective engagement with shareholders.

- Each of our stakeholders is essential. We commit to deliver value to all of them, for the future success of our companies, our communities, and our country.

What the Harvard study revealed is that, despite BR's corporate governance guidance, there was very little change to signatory companies' board structure or other obvious public documents in the span of one year.

Which is to be expected.

Because real structural, organizational change is hard and complicated. Because actually living up to a greater purpose requires more than signing a statement of intent but the hard work of determining how a brand will deliver on a purpose promise that is both unique and universal.

What I've learned in the last 15 years of sustainability consulting and more than 30 years as a communicator is that all change is behavior change. It's a head and heart journey. It takes vision—where are we headed? It takes heart—how will we feel when facing the challenge of change? And it takes intelligence—what are the facts we need to know, how do we quantify what's hard to do, how do we measure how far we've come?

The problem with the Harvard study one year after the BR commitment is that it looked at only one dimension of change—board governance. An important aspect to be sure. Governance and structure at the highest levels of accountability within companies are critical components of finding and living a brand purpose that serves the needs of all stakeholders. But sometimes change comes from other places in the organization.

There is a phrase in community organizing about the "grassroots and grass tops." Real change needs both. Momentum can come from the top—a CEO who has had an epiphany like Ray Anderson of Interface (see the following case study). Or sustainability programs can come from unofficial "green" teams within companies who start by simply self-organizing recycling or food waste programs inside their companies because they see a need.

No matter where the seeds of change come from, the grassroots eventually must meet the grass tops to affect the full system change needed to deliver on purpose's intention.

Since 2019 we have seen a sea change in attention for corporate purpose, a tidal wave of corporate commitments and an explosion of ESG-indicated funds as well as the rapid growth of impact investing.

Purpose also began dominating marketing conversations and now is an important aspiration for thousands of brands. In a rapidly changing post-Covid and climate-change world, where so much has shifted and the world continues to grapple with the effects of societal unrest, purpose has become the expression of an ideal that has found its moment.

The Story of Ray Anderson and Interface

When I began my sustainability education in the mid 2000s, there were no sustainability MBAs, no degrees in environmental management. The fastest way to become adept as a practitioner was to read every book available on the subject, attend conferences, conduct interviews with those tackling sustainability inside early movers, and seek out certifications or other fragmented programs that provided insights into what parts of the business where the most material change needed to happen.

I met Ray Andersen, late founder and chairman of Interface Inc., one of the world's largest manufacturers of commercial and residential carpet, in 2009. He was already a hero of mine thanks to the visionary work he led at Interface as described in his book, *Confessions of a Radical Industrialist*. His 2009 TED Talk will give you everything you need to know about the soul and smarts of this environmental leader who has inspired generations of business leaders. "Because if we can do it, anyone can do it. And if anyone can do it, everyone must do it" (Anderson, 2009). It's amazing to watch that video and see how the CEO of a petroleum-based B2B company was one of the first to deploy systems thinking in addressing the impact his company was having on the planet and commit to a net-zero future. His mathematical equation for assessing impact was beautiful in its simplicity. He shows how the next technology revolution must include "more happiness with less stuff." Ray Anderson is a beautiful example of vision from the grass tops.

Defining Purpose

To understand what purpose is, it's important to define and distinguish it from a company's mission and vision statements. Purpose also has interplay with sustainability and ESG programs.

Purpose is a company's understanding and articulation of the greater good it wants to create in the world, using its business as a mechanism for delivering a regenerative planet and an equitable society. A company's purpose usually is focused primarily on either environmental or social outcomes but always takes into consideration the intersectional nature of both.

Companies who understand this, understand that they exist beyond the singular interest of shareholders and delivering shareholder value. Companies that understand purpose realize that they must take responsibility for their impact on the planet and society.

Purpose goes beyond an organizational self-interest of "it's got to be primarily good for the company" where purpose efforts must serve all of their value directly to the company. True purpose looks beyond the company, beyond the industry and looks at the whole. At the commons.

I use the term "commons" to describe what every company, every individual has a responsibility to protect and nurture. The commons are all the resources we depend upon but none of us own. The commons is an expression of the collective that works for all of us.

When I talk about a company's purpose, what I'm looking for is, does a company understand how it can take the vast resources it has control over—everything from dozens to hundreds of thousands of employees, millions of customers, everything it buys—and orient all of those in service to some greater good? In service to protecting or nurturing the commons? When you think about the sheer scale of all the dimensions of a corporation and how they can be deployed toward preserving the planet and society alongside delivering business value, then you clearly understand purpose.

The Three Elements of Purpose

- **Essence:** The unique brand attributes and qualities that make your company unique.
- **Hope:** A vision for a thriving future.
- **Resource:** The environmental or social asset that your company will take responsibility for protecting and nurturing

Purposeful brands hold these three distinct characteristics in an integrated, interrelated truth.

The first element of an effective and authentic purpose is a strong brand expression, a company's essence. "Companies who know who they are, know what to do," says my colleague Cali Pitchell, with whom I have collaborated on a range of purpose exploration projects. I love this insight because it starts at the heart of any successful company, its brand. We define a brand as more than just the logo or mark, but the entire expression of a company's mission in a unique way. There are hundreds of books, podcasts and talks on brand strategy with MBA and design school coursework dedicated to teaching techniques for developing a comprehensive brand expression. Essentially, brand guidelines are the internal document that capture in one place what makes a company different:

- visual identity (logo, colors, fonts, graphic universe)
- editorial identity (tone of voice, keywords, communication and expression formats)
- mission statement, history, and values (the story of what the company exists to do as a business)
- products and services (what it does and how it delivers on its promised value)

The second element of purpose is hope. Purpose is defined as the reason for which something is done or created, or for which something exists. It also is an objective or intention. Intentions is a word I use often to describe how best to articulate purpose in exploration sessions. This second purpose element should unlock creativity, a sense of what's possible. What do we intend? What future state do we imagine? What would this purpose give us permission to do that we don't already do? What does it allow us to say no to? Where might our business, our sector, our world be in the next generation or seven generations? What all these questions depend upon is an interior sense of hope, of a better future. Which, frankly, is at the heart of every founder's story or is the motivation of every entrepreneur.

The final element of purpose is an understanding of the resource, either environmental or social, that your brand is committed to preserving or nurturing. Depending upon the sector your business operates in, there will be a natural focus area that is most relevant. This is part operational, part market focus and customer need, and part leader and employee passion. Sometimes the company's purpose can be discovered by digging into the founder's story. Many times, the passion of the inventor or original entrepreneur who wanted to make lives easier, solve an operational challenge, or meet a customer requirement is a good place to start.

Take a look at Coca-Cola. On their company website, they have a clearly articulated purpose: Refresh the World. Make a Difference. The founder's story is also prominent:

> The product that has given the world its best-known taste was born in Atlanta, Georgia, on May 8, 1886. Dr. John Stith Pemberton, a local pharmacist, produced the syrup for Coca-Cola, and carried a jug of the new product down the street to Jacobs' Pharmacy, where it was sampled, pronounced "excellent" and placed on sale for five cents a glass as a soda fountain drink. Carbonated water was teamed with the new syrup to produce a drink that was at once "Delicious and Refreshing," a theme that continues to echo today wherever Coca-Cola is enjoyed.
>
> (Coca-Cola, 2022)

The choice of "Refresh the World" as the first half of their purpose statement is clearly linked to the earliest days of the company. It also gives them space to define "refresh" in how they address their environmental footprint. It can also provide some flexibility for programs and efforts to restore people as well as the planet. The world (environment) is the shared resource they are committed to preserving, to making better. That's a tough assignment for Coca-Cola as activists at COP27 called out the conference's acceptance of sponsorship funds from the beverage company as greenwashing. Sometimes, the hardest commitment to make is one that is at the heart of the business. For Coca-Cola, changing its role as the top plastic polluter is central to its business, its reputation and its purpose (Green and McVeigh, 2022).

The Commons and Tragedy

I was first introduced to the concept of the commons in Jane Jacob's 1961 ground-breaking book, *The Death and Life of Great American Cities*, where she presented a damning critique of traditional urban planning and the antisocial effects of skyscrapers and abstract aesthetic principles. She presented an argument for the perspective that should be at the heart of all urban design—centering it on the community who actually lives in an urban neighborhood. The commons as she expresses in her book is the ephemeral idea of community cohesion and quality of life that design realities can either nurture or destroy. She realized that community is not an abstract design principle but rather is an everyday lived experience and should be a central force in urban design. A revolutionary concept for its time.

This brought into stark relief for me the idea that there are shared resources that all of us depend upon but none of us own. We all intuitively understand that air, water, and even the richness of soil are natural resources that are critical to our human existence as well as that of the species with whom we share the planet.

The "Aha" for me in Jacob's book was that our shared social experience is also part of the commons. I also realized that institutions and cultural norms could either support or dismantle our societal fabric. The last few years have only reinforced how misinformation and social mores can unintentionally, or perhaps intentionally, create divisiveness and break down the cohesion we need to ensure a thriving planet and an equitable society.

It's an awareness that business leaders are clearly also seeing. Research from Porter Novelli in 2021 revealed that 93 percent of executives recognize that addressing societal issues is now part of running a successful business. A challenge, to be sure, since the same research indicates that more than three-quarters (77 percent) say it is hard to balance the need to address societal issues with the need to make a profit (Porter Novelli, 2021a).

Paired with the idea of the commons, is a term that has widespread application and is linked to sustainability—"the tragedy of the commons." The concept became widely known thanks to an article in

1968 by ecologist Garrett Hardin entitled "The tragedy of the commons," published in the journal *Science*.

This theory explains individuals' tendency to make the best decisions for their personal situation. In Hardin's article, he cited an example from an 1833 pamphlet by English economist William Forster Lloyd of overgrazing privately owned cattle in the village's shared green space, without regard to the negative impact this may have on others' need to graze their cattle as well. For a current example of the tragedy of the commons, we can see people acting with their short-term best interest in mind when they use plastic shopping bags and disregard the well-known harm plastic can cause the environment.

We can also see that when companies protect their business at the expense of deliberately and knowingly harming shared resources, more scrutiny and backlash are the result. One sector that is under increased pressure is the fossil fuel industry. There is a growing realization that the industry has a history of climate misinformation, similar to that of the tobacco industry.

In mid 2021, there were 1,841 ongoing or concluded climate litigation cases around the world, with legal developments on the rise. There were more cases, a total of 191, filed during 2020 than the 170 lawsuits filed from 2015 to 2019 combined. In addition to an increase in cases, the past five years has also seen the addition of lawsuits relating to the role of public relations (PR) and advertising in climate change. PR and advertising agencies are being accused of working with fossil fuel companies to spread climate disinformation, creating significant reputational, business, and legal risk. Key players are no longer limited to just those companies doing the actual extraction; they now include those who participate in false narratives that destroy ecosystems (CleanCreatives, 2022).

What's true for grazing greens, oceans, or rain forests is also true for democracies and neighborhoods, for indigenous lands and ethnic communities, for healthy families and digitally literate children.

More and more brand leaders are expressing a sense of responsibility for closing the digital divide, supporting Black entrepreneurs, recognizing lesbian, gay, bisexual, transgender, queer (and others) (LGBTQ+) rights and a range of other commitments.

All reveal a growing cadre of next generation companies who are protecting our environmental and societal commons from tragedy. Who understand that purpose is at the heart of why business exists.

In a recent *Harvard Business Review* article, authors Jonathan Knowles, B Tom Hunsaker, Hannah Grove, and Alison James share, "Our research indicates that a primary cause of this confusion is that 'purpose' is used in three senses: competence ('the function that our product serves'); culture ('the intent with which we run our business'); and cause ('the social good to which we aspire')" (Knowles et al, 2022).

This quote gives us a good place to begin deconstructing purpose and its interplay with mission and values and how to understand the expectations that are coming from all sides and all stakeholders. The authors have posited that purpose has three different meanings, but I would define what they see as three various takes on purpose as actually good definitions for mission, values, and purpose.

Mission

As the HBR authors define competence, it is "the function that our product serves." I see this as a brand's mission. A mission helps employees remain focused on the tasks at hand and encourages them to find innovative ways of moving toward increasing their productivity with the eye to achieving company goals. Mission statements describe how companies will serve customers and make their lives better. Included in mission statements are usually details about what market a business is in, the approach it will take, and a future seen for the business.

When differentiating from purpose, mission statements are specific to the business itself and the way it will deliver value to customers. Purpose statements describe how companies will use their focus and assets to benefit the commons, the greater good.

Table 1.1 lists a few examples from well-known brands who have clearly differentiated mission and purpose statements.

Table 1.1   Example purpose statements from well-known brands

Company	Mission	Purpose
Nordstrom	We exist to help our customers feel good and look their best.	We remain committed to leaving the world better than we found it.
Ikea	To offer a wide range of well-designed, functional home furnishing products at prices so low that as many people as possible will be able to afford them.	To create a better everyday life for the many people.
Sony	Our mission is to be a company that inspires and fulfills your curiosity.	Creating a world filled with emotion. For the next generation.
Procter & Gamble	We will provide branded products and services of superior quality and value...	...that improve the lives of the world's consumers, now and for generations to come.

Some companies are what I call "born green" brands, which is short-hand for a company that was founded with a mission that is a true purpose. These companies are designed to both provide a product or service and deliver a benefit to stakeholders and ecosystems well beyond their four walls.

Patagonia is a great example of a purpose-driven company. Their mission statement is also their purpose. They do not need two statements since they have organized the company's business, advocacy, marketing, and communications around a singular concept: "We're in business to save our home planet."

When we unpack this statement, it is important to look back into the company's founding story and see how their business strategy has evolved in alignment with a commitment to the planet, even if it has not always been explicitly stated. That is the hallmark of a born green brand.

For every company in Table 1.1, you will see a focus that tends to be more oriented to supporting a flourishing planet or an equitable society. This makes sense when you realize that a brand's purpose is an expression of how the very business itself will organize its assets, resources, stakeholders, and products as expressed in a shared value for a positive outcome. When the purpose statement is carefully crafted, it can then cascade to inform sustainability strategy (both environmental and social) and the ESG programs that deliver on strategy and purpose.

Purpose is also not a marketing strategy or a communications technique. When done authentically, it drives business strategy and unlocks creativity, innovation, and stakeholder engagement. Customers want to buy from purposeful brands, employees want to work for them, investors want to support expansion, and regulators look to align regulatory constraints, while NGOs and nonprofits partner to support a shared theory of change.

Purpose is the word we use to define an organization's "why." It sits alongside the "what." What a company makes or the service it provides. It is also more than the "how" which specifies an approach that's unique—innovation, value, efficiency, price. Purpose is bigger than a brand's self-interest and is an expression of the authentic and distinctive strengths it will bring to the planet or society.

I see campaigns and admonitions from experts that brands need to authentically engage with communities and causes as an expression of purpose but also to ensure connections that can benefit the organization with new customers, increased market share and other business drivers. I am not suggesting that driving growth is not an essential outcome of a defined purpose. It is. But when you set and articulate a purpose that is bigger, more expansive, it generates momentum that will drive engagement, loyalty, and expansion. It's like the adage that financials are a trailing indicator that you have taken care of your employees and your customers. When you have a clear and inspiring purpose, you invite others to join you on your journey to a better world, a better business.

Values

Values are an important part of the trifecta of mission, values, and purpose. When carefully articulated, values give employees an understanding of the behaviors that are expected of them that will lead to success—for themselves, the organization, and the greater good that the company aims to achieve.

Values are usually created by the chief human resources officer (CHRO) in collaboration with a diverse group of company leaders including the CEO, senior executives, brand and marketing leaders, and key employee groups. In its values, a company can express its personality, its soul, its human dimension in ways that tell all its stakeholders—not just its employees—what to expect from interactions between and among everyone the company depends upon for its success.

A good example of unique and differentiated values are those at Airbnb. These playfully express the ways in which employees can show up, participate, and drive the Airbnb mission to "Create a world where anyone can belong anywhere." Values are a way to express culture and invite a wide range of stakeholders to see themselves in how the brand operates. And while Airbnb does not have an explicitly stated purpose statement, I think its mission does a good job of articulating the greater societal good that Airbnb is aiming to serve. They exist to create "belonging" for everyone so they can experience the world in a more authentic, connected way.

Airbnb's values:

- champion the mission (by living the mission)
- be a host
- simplify
- every frame matters
- be a cereal entrepreneur
- embrace the adventure

According to their website, Airbnb began in "2007 when two Hosts welcomed three guests to their San Francisco home and has since grown to 4 million Hosts who have welcomed more than 1 billion guest arrivals in almost every country across the globe." Because they are still so close to the beginning, the original passion and creativity that the founders deployed to create a greater good is still closely integrated into how the company behaves and tells its story. It's why some born green brands don't have a specific purpose statement—because the origins contain the company's intention and soul.

How Do Purpose, Sustainability, and ESG Work Together?

We've defined purpose as the commitment a brand makes to ensuring a thriving planet and an equitable society by taking its vast resources—employees, customers, resources, influence—and orienting them in service to some greater good.

Many people think purpose is a fad that will quickly fade. I think it reflects people's growing understanding of the interdependence between commerce, society, and planetary resources. For too long, thanks to Friedman, we saw business as separate from both the social constructs and infrastructure it needs to operate (roads, water, energy grids, stable societies) and the natural resources extracted or harvested with no thought for long-term effects.

Whether it is weather events that are either disrupting supply chains and damaging manufacturing facilities or preventing customers from accessing goods, or social unrest caused by hate crimes or political backlash, brands are waking up to the reality of systems thinking. Of the need to protect and nurture the commons rather than quickly exploit for self-interested gain. Whether we continue to call that purpose or simple better business, time will tell.

Another confusion is that many believe purpose is interchangeable with sustainability and ESG. Over the years, I have developed a clear understanding of how they must be distinct yet interconnected to drive change and value across a brand's stakeholder matrix (Figure 1.1).

Figure 1.1   Integration of purpose with sustainability, ESG, and communications

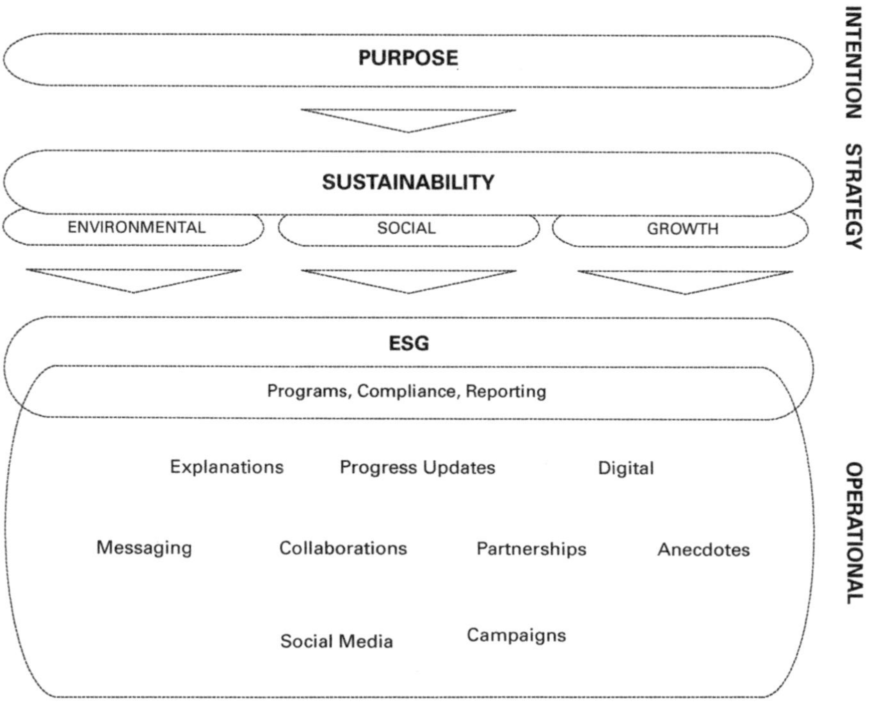

Defining Sustainability

Sustainability became a mainstream concept in the 1980s when the United Nations Brundtland Commission referred to it as "meeting our own needs without compromising the ability of future generations to meet their own needs." Since then, scientists, sociologists, economists, and experts across many other fields have come to look at sustainability practices in three dimensions: environmental, economic, and social.

From a purposeful brand perspective, sustainability holds the operational strategy that a company will deploy to manage its environmental and social impacts in a way that allows for financial stability. It is the way in which the brand will operationalize its purpose and create shared value for all stakeholders. It will also guide decisions for how the company will manage the entirety of its value chain— some of which indirectly deliver on purpose but nonetheless must be carefully directed to ensure the least harmful impacts.

> Transforming businesses to respect environmental limits while fulfilling social wants and needs has become an unparalleled platform for innovation on strategy, design, manufacturing and brand—offering massive opportunities to compete and to adapt in a rapidly evolving world.
>
> (KoAnn Skryzinyaz, Founder and CEO, Sustainable Brands)

There are three essential elements in sustainability:

- Environmental practices are centered around preserving and protecting natural resources, reducing waste, and only consuming what can be replenished.
- Economic practices are focused on nurturing profitability and growth today and for future generations, such as building carbon-neutral offices or adopting technology that will create energy efficiencies throughout our cities.
- Social practices are concentrated on ensuring that everyone has their basic needs met and that communities are kept safe, secure, healthy, and happy.

Environment, Social, Governance

Purpose and ESG are related, and sometimes the initiatives associated with each will overlap. While purpose is about joint value creation between business and the planet/society, ESG is more about managing downside risk. ESG contains a rigorous methodology for calculating and reporting on a company's environmental commitments, progress, and challenges as well as human capital dimensions like diversity and inclusion, and societal issues like equity and justice.

From net-zero commitments to diversity targets, from packaging innovation and zero waste to landfill to human rights policies, brands have a far-reaching set of activities that can have either positive or negative outcomes on the planet and society. A comprehensive ESG program, which ladders up to clear sustainability goals and vision, has now been proven to be a consistent predictor of a well-run company—one that carefully manages its resources, reduces expensive waste, has minimal staff churn thanks to talent management and DEI programs that create a welcoming culture, and has the expansive policies, commitments, and organizational structure in place to ensure consistency in delivering strong ESG/sustainability results.

If purpose expresses a brand's responsibility to a wide range of stakeholders, how can we understand what these stakeholders expect from companies? Porter Novelli research, conducted for over thirty years on the attitudes and expectations of customers, investors, and the general public, has uncovered a shifting set of expectations for businesses, governments, and NGOs. A Porter Novelli study of "C-suite" executive-level managers reveals that a new generation of leaders understand that tackling issues beyond profit is paramount to effective performance (Porter Novelli, 2021a):

- 95 percent of business executives say it is more important to them now than in the past to understand the needs and concerns of all their stakeholders.

- 82 percent say it is challenging to know if, when, and how to address hot-button societal issues, with a further 87 percent insisting they need more resources or counsel to navigate the societal issues they face today.

- 74 percent say shareholders are no longer their single most important stakeholders.

New leaders can infuse the personal with the professional and authentically consider what matters to all stakeholders by understanding how impacting societal issues can be an effective way to drive long-term business value. This new path is not easy—and many executives are the first to admit they need help in achieving it. In today's culturally conscious society, successful leaders are the ones who are deeply curious about the needs of their stakeholders and are always listening to the latest marketplace intelligence—not just business intelligence—but social and emotional intelligence as well.

The business leaders of today acknowledge that strong support is needed to align on that vision as well as execute action that will lead to both business and societal results. And the chief communications officer (CCO) is poised to play a critical role in helping executives wade these waters. Business leaders were united (97 percent) in their belief that the CCO is more important to their organization than in the past—and nearly 40 percent say that the CCO is the most important internal stakeholder whose input matters when navigating today's business issues. A further 96 percent of leaders see communications as an increasingly critical part of the company sales and marketing mix. This shows a nuance in how executives are looking to lead in the marketplace—through deep stakeholder intelligence and thoughtful and focused communications around a strong corporate vision.

These emerging leaders who are listening to stakeholder voices are paying attention to research that shows customers and future employees—mostly Millennials and Gen Z—expect more from the products they buy and the companies who make them.

According to SB Brands for Good, 96 percent of US consumers said they try to live sustainable lifestyles at least some of the time and 85 percent say they are loyal to brands that help them to achieve a better and more balanced life. This is the case for expectation on companies to show up in support of social issues as well (SB Brands for Good, 2021).

While traditionally defined as more pragmatic and rational than their Millennial peers, Gen Z emerged in the mid 2010s with an energy, enthusiasm, and a demand for the world to acknowledge that change needs to happen fast. This cohort was thrust into a series of increasingly urgent crises—from a global pandemic to calls for racial justice in the United States. Watching government and corporate response to these challenges hit and miss, Gen Z's trust in institutions has diminished.

According to Porter Novelli's Gen Z social justice and corporate reputation study:

> When it comes to company engagement in social justice, Gen Zers are less inspired by words, but motivated by action. They're willing to do their homework but slightly less willing to forgive a corporate misstep. And as this generation moves into the workforce, they are strongly

considering a company's approach to social justice and are even willing to leave a current job if they feel their employer hasn't done enough to address these issues.

(Porter Novelli, 2021b)

When a company's purpose is deeply embedded and not just superficial, when it is enduring and not ephemeral, stakeholders will buy from, work for, or invest in this new generation of purposeful brands.

References

Anderson, R (2009) The business logic of sustainability, TED, www.ted.com/talks/ray_anderson_the_business_logic_of_sustainability (archived at https://perma.cc/X93F-VQLG)

Bebchuk, L and Tallarita, R (2020) The illusory promise of stakeholder governance, Harvard Law School Forum on Corporate Governance, https://corpgov.law.harvard.edu/2020/03/02/the-illusory-promise-of-stakeholder-governance (archived at https://perma.cc/J7BQ-GB3B)

BlackRock (2019) Larry Fink's letter to CEOs, BlackRock, www.blackrock.com/americas-offshore/en/2019-larry-fink-ceo-letter (archived at https://perma.cc/S94J-2NAQ)

Business Roundtable (2019) Business Roundtable redefines the purpose of a corporation to promote 'an economy that serves all Americans', Business Roundtable, www.businessroundtable.org/business-roundtable-redefines-the-purpose-of-a-corporation-to-promote-an-economy-that-serves-all-americans (archived at https://perma.cc/UAX8-4Q9A)

CleanCreatives (2022) Smoke and mirrors: The legal risks of fossil fuel advertising, CleanCreatives, https://cleancreatives.org/smoke-and-mirrors (archived at https://perma.cc/RF7B-QK84)

Coca-Cola (2022) The birth of a refreshing idea, Coca-Cola, www.coca-colacompany.com/company/history/the-birth-of-a-refreshing-idea (archived at https://perma.cc/F6J2-TVJZ)

Green, G and McVeigh, K (2022) Cop27 climate summit's sponsorship by Coca-Cola condemned as 'greenwash', *Guardian*, www.theguardian.com/environment/2022/oct/04/cop27-climate-summit-sponsorship-polluter-coca-cola-condemned-as-greenwash (archived at https://perma.cc/WYW2-JHY7)

Hardin, G (1968) The tragedy of the commons, *Science*, 162 (3859), 1243–48

Knowles, J, Hunsaker, B T, Grove, H, and James, A (2022) What is the purpose of your purpose? *Harvard Business Review*, https://hbr.org/2022/03/what-is-the-purpose-of-your-purpose (archived at https://perma.cc/2CTX-RA7E)

Porter Novelli (2021a) The 2021 Porter Novelli executive influence study, PN, www.porternovelli.com/findings/the-2021-porter-novelli-executive-influence-study (archived at https://perma.cc/Z4HL-J2KW)

Porter Novelli (2021b) 2021 Porter Novelli focus: Gen Z and justice, PN, www.porternovelli.com/findings/2021-porter-novelli-focus-gen-z-justice (archived at https://perma.cc/K9CE-TZFD)

SB Brands for Good (2021) Socio-cultural trends: Understand consumer intentions and actions towards sustainable lifestyles, SB Brands for Good, https://sbbrandsforgood.com/socio-cultural-trends (archived at https://perma.cc/J5Q4-R68H)

Sorkin, A R and de la Merced, M J (2019) It's not 'woke' for businesses to think beyond profit, BlackRock chief says, *New York Times*, www.nytimes.com/2019/01/17/business/dealbook/blackrock-larry-fink-letter.html (archived at https://perma.cc/L53S-SW37)

Articulating Your Purpose

02

Exploring and Defining Your North Star With a "Yes—and" Mindset

Every business purpose journey is also a personal journey. Throughout my work with executives, helping them explore how to find and articulate a North Star for their companies, I am also privileged to hear personal "Aha" moments. We all have had that moment when we see the world differently, when some unseen truth reveals itself. Many are waking up to how we can have greater impact through our work. The same was true for me.

The ampersand is my favorite symbol and "Yes—and" is my life philosophy. So, what does "Yes—and" look like? It looks like the good, Midwestern, Catholic girl I was. I married my college boyfriend, started my communications career, and had two beautiful little girls. Then, like half of the US, I got divorced. After years as a single mom, I met the love of my life. And then I married her.

And even though, for me, everything in my life seemed exactly the same—I had a spouse, kids, a great career, family vacations—nothing was the same. Not in the mid 1990s when I came out. I quickly discovered that by being married to a woman, I was often marginalized by the very system that I had been comfortably inhabiting.

I began to see that the institutions I had taken for granted—like marriage and a heteronormative workplace where sharing news about your spouse felt comfortable didn't make room for me now that I was suddenly outside of the system—a lesbian, married to a woman.

It's strange, but coming out in my mid-thirties gave me the gift of insight. Because I saw how false social constructs really are. When you are forced out of your place in the world, you see that there is benefit in interrogating the status quo and you get to see reality from a different perspective—one that is more inclusive and adaptive. One that sees the invisible—homophobia, structural misogyny, institutional racism, privilege, and climate change.

My "Aha" moment 25 years ago made me a "Yes—and" thinker. A nonbinary thinker. Nonbinary thinking means having the capacity to embrace the truth of what is seen and what is invisible. To see what is broken and how to pivot to what's possible. To see that almost all of reality exists on a spectrum from one gradation to the other. "Yes—and" or nonbinary thinking is the single most important aspect for building a purposeful brand.

Ray Anderson called these "Aha" moments a "spear in the chest" epiphany. That moment when something true is revealed that cannot be unseen. One CEO I worked with at an outdoor apparel company spoke of his moment. It came while listening to a Black colleague describe the pain and fear he experienced following George Floyd's death. Floyd was a Black American murdered in 2020 by a police officer in Minneapolis, Minnesota during an arrest for the possible use of a counterfeit twenty-dollar bill.

This CEO, who was leading his company's purpose exploration, had been looking only at the environmental dimension of their footprint but, after listening to his employee describe in such stark reality what it means to be Black in America, he was, in his words, changed forever. As I worked with his team, I was struck by how much emotional intelligence and empathy he displayed and how he stepped back so that those most affected could step forward and help design and articulate a brand purpose that promises to act so that everyone can access the outdoors—safely and freely.

Defining a brand's purpose takes the ability to hold two seemingly disparate positions. You must be able to hold business challenges and possibility in tension with social or environmental issues and opportunities. To find the blue-sky space where a brand's uniqueness and resources can be brought to bear in a place of need.

eBay is a great example of this. eBay's real founding story is not as well-known as the one fabricated about a Pez dispenser collection belonging to Pierre Omidyar's wife. He actually spent a Labor Day weekend on his personal computer to create Auction Web, a site "dedicated to bringing together buyers and sellers in an honest and open market-place" (eBay, 2022). But it does show how a business innovation can become a purpose that solves an environmental or social problem. In the early days at eBay, according to an interview with Omidyar on the company's website, they worked to keep up with demand as more and more people saw two things about eBay they wanted to participate in: (1) reselling as a way to gain financial advantage and (2) keep useful items from the landfill. The twin benefits of entrepreneurship and circularity remain as the core elements of the company's purpose, sustainability strategy, and ESG programs (eBay, 2022). More later on how those are all integrated and serve to help a brand deliver outcomes that benefit the environment or society.

> ### Companies must be a force for growth and a force for good.
> Marc Pritchard, Chief Brand Officer, Porter & Gamble (Aziz, 2019)

As we discussed in the first chapter, purpose has evolved as a business term over the years, and many times it gets conflated with brand mission or vision. In my experience, and given the continued exploration of what stakeholders expect of companies, purpose is now an expression of the greater good a company will create in the world *as* a business. A business is an entity that exists to sell a product or service at a profit, in a way that protects the environment for all future generations and species.

When purpose is limited to defining only a business outcome, brands can miss a richer, more dimensional understanding of why they exist. Interestingly, in 1960, HP's co-founder David Packard gave a speech to managers explaining his belief about why companies exist that I think is closest to what I believe is a purposeful brand:

I think many people assume, wrongly, that a company exists simply to make money. While this is an important result of a company's existence, we have to go deeper and find the real reasons for our being. As we investigate this, we inevitably come to the conclusion that a group of people get together and exist as an institution that we call a company so they are able to accomplish something collectively that they could not accomplish separately—they make a contribution to society, a phrase which sounds trite but is fundamental.

(Jones, 2016)

Unpacking this reveals two separate but intertwined concepts: (1) collective effort, and (2) contribution to society (i.e., a greater good). I like hearing that David Packard was interested in exploring a reason for being that contributed to society's well-being, even if he felt the need to characterize it as trite. What we've all come to understand in a rapidly heating up world with glaring inequalities driving conflict, ensuring businesses explore their reason for being is a critical next-level understanding of the role of commerce and capitalism.

I've seen a host of diagrams and schematics that try to explain the relationship between purpose and business objectives and think what's needed is a simplification which shows where purpose sits within operational dimensions, customer requirements and external realities. When a company has a clearly articulated purpose sitting at the center, it cascades out across every operational silo, beginning with the C-suite and moving through departments, executed as part of an ESG strategy, and finds its impacts and outcomes in ecosystems and socio-cultural institutions (Figure 2.1).

One example of how a clearly defined brand purpose might play out operationally can be found in work we did with a technology company that manufacturers computers, laptops, and enterprise hardware. Executives in the marketing and sustainability departments who were responsible for brand strategy, social programs, philanthropy, and go-to-market strategies were looking for an authentic and expansive way to lead in support for closing the digital divide. They recognized, as most technology companies do, that access to devices and infrastructure is just the first step in lifting people and communities out of poverty and into prosperity. People and organizations also need digital literacy, financial support, unrestricted data access, continuing education, and access to the internet and electricity. Along with many of their competitors, they decided that access would be their purpose.

Figure 2.1   Purpose at the center is operationalized across silos

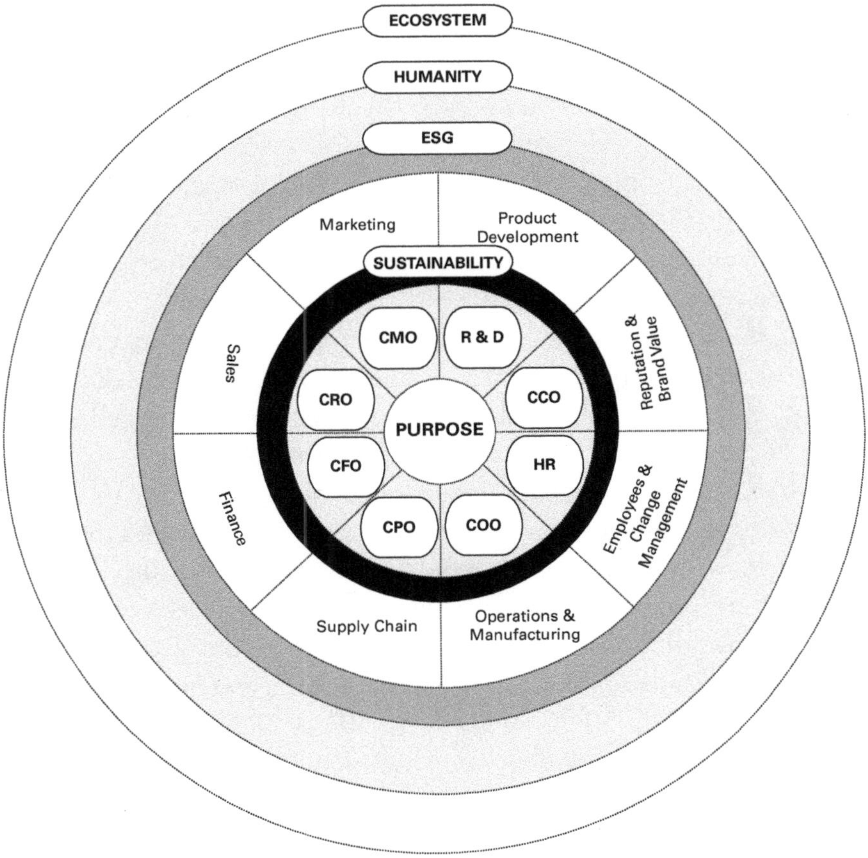

But what did they mean by access? Initially, it was all about giving newly outdated laptops and equipment to communities in developing nations and sponsoring technology classes in economically challenged neighborhoods. Nothing wrong with these efforts, but hardly inspiring or broad enough to be deployed across an entire company.

There is a set of questions I like to pose as the beginning of any purpose engagement with a brand. It starts with an open-ended query. Does the world need what you are making? This question gets to the heart of a brand's why. There are some products that, once we explore all that it takes to produce an object, find that its essential purpose is diminished.

The next set of questions began to get at the greater areas for exploration which led to a unique expression of access from the technology company described earlier. Who makes your products? Who are you making them for? Are you leaving anyone out? What are you making them with? What happens to them after they no longer work?

When we took a step back and looked at access from a fresh perspective, specifically from the lens of disability access, the team had an "Aha" moment. What if we take on access to the digital world for those with disabilities as an expression of our purpose? This unlocked an enthusiastic and creative conversation about all that was now possible: They could become the best-in-class innovator at making technology accessible to people of every ability. They could look at who makes their products and see how they might source labor from people currently marginalized because of their physical abilities. They could expand research to better understand neuro differences and leverage those learnings to design workplaces and physical environments across office campuses that nurture the many ways that people process information, socialize, collaborate, and are productive. Once we introduced the concept of purpose orienting toward full access supporting the widest possible spectrum of physical and neuro abilities, creativity, enthusiasm, and innovation, conversations blossomed.

Right away, the marketing and sustainability leaders were joined by operations, human resources (HR), procurement, facilities, research and development (R&D), and product design in imagining how they could operationalize access, regardless of abilities, into varying facets of their business.

Purpose Exploration

Articulating a brand's purpose, or North Star, can be accomplished through a proven methodology that I have used for many companies. In each case, we were looking for an expression of purpose that did three things: (1) it was intrinsically and authentically tied to the business and its mission to deliver what its customers wanted and needed; (2) the purpose was connected to an environmental or social need/opportunity that was integral to the business; and (3) it helped further amplify and express the brand itself, its legacy, persona, and uniqueness.

The three-phased process starts with a deep *discovery* and analysis, followed by *ideation* and creation of a purpose statement and manifesto that expresses the emotional dimensionality. Purpose exploration concludes with a programmatic *plan* that captures how it cascades across all dimensions of the business and is interwoven seamlessly into all communications platforms and campaigns.

There are four aspects to the discovery phase that provide a brand with everything it needs to know when exploring how to discern and express its purpose. This is probably one of the most important phases, but not the hardest one. The second phase, ideation, is where a brand synthesizes everything it learned in discovery and it's the most difficult because it requires a clear-eyed understanding of what is true to the company and where its real opportunity for change and contribution lies.

Discovery

Let's start with the four aspects of discovery and take a close look at each one.

1. Company Audit

Origin Exploration

Starting with the origin story, a close look at the founders, the early product formulations, the lore, and mystery of the brand's earliest market successes are a wonderful place to start. It is important to do this in an unvarnished way. To not sugarcoat the challenges or mistakes. To not avoid looking at the missteps and controversies throughout the company's history. How brands respond to challenge and disaster are key ingredients to unlocking a purpose. Sometimes a purpose becomes the way in which a company will show up in the world or society regardless of what product or service it is offering. Take Ikea: "A better life for the many people" is based on a statement its founder, Ingvar Kamprad, made in the 1940s while the brand was still a furniture company based in rural Sweden. The statement reflects the humble, early roots of the company while hinting at its modern focus: sustainability.

Materiality Assessment

The next area of exploration is a deep dive into what the company is actually delivering from a sustainability perspective as expressed in the ESG programs and reports. What we are looking for here is a close examination of a brand's say/do gap. As a company looks closer at expressing a purpose beyond profit, a way of showing up in the world that contributes to a healthier ecosystem or a more equitable society, the first place any of us will look is inside their business. How are they treating employees? Are the products made responsibly? Is the management team diverse? How well is the company doing in delivering value to its customers and profits to its shareholders?

The answers to these questions are usually found in a materiality assessment—a common sustainability process that companies use to prioritize the issues and concerns that intersect across business, environmental, and social dimensions. A good materiality assessment, usually conducted by the sustainability department, creates a prioritized list of both risks and opportunities that affect both the company's social license to operate and critical vulnerabilities that pose both an operational and reputational risk to a brand. A materiality assessment helps an organization identify, affirm, and prioritize the ESG issues that are the most critical to their business. It is the starting point for a structured sustainability strategy, clarifying focus, goals, broad key performance indicators (KPIs), and priorities. It ensures careful consideration of the risk, capital, and brand value dimensions of ESG/sustainability strategy.

An interesting development in materiality assessments is the move from single materiality to double materiality. Single refers to a close look at the issues, challenges, and risks that a company faces to its business. This can include unstable supply chains or lack of access to raw materials. It can also be regulatory expectations regarding a company's responsibility to protect and preserve personal information and data privacy. Or perhaps it is rising fuel prices and the cost of transportation. All of these are environmental or social dimensions that create risk profiles that a company's enterprise risk management department is constantly pulsing. Essentially, what impact is the world (environmentally or socially) having on the business?

Double materiality refers to the impact that the business has on the environment and society alongside the effects that the environment and society have on the business. How do the actions of a company affect air quality via its greenhouse gas emissions? What are the parameters of pay equity or worker safety within the company and the communities where it runs manufacturing or warehouse operations?

According to the United States Securities and Exchange Commission (SEC):

> [A] matter is "material" if there is a substantial likelihood that a reasonable person would consider it important... The omission or misstatement of an item is material if, in the light of the surrounding circumstances, the magnitude of the item is such that it is probable that the judgment of a reasonable person relying on the information would have been changed or influenced by the inclusion or correction of the item.
>
> (Securities and Exchange Commission, 1999)

To further elaborate, Global Reporting Initiative (2021) explains that "material topics are topics that reflect the organization's most significant impacts on the economy, environment, and people, including impacts on human rights." Starting in 2023, companies operating in the European Union (EU) will need to incorporate double materiality into their sustainability reporting. The discipline of materiality assessments takes into consideration the fact that what is material for one company in a particular industry will not be the same for another company.

Retailers have different physical footprints than clothing companies. Food manufacturers have a completely different set of material issues—soil health, water use, animal welfare, food safety, worker safety and labor rights, energy use, packaging, transportation—than a bank or a software company with a remote workforce.

So, a materiality assessment that prioritizes ESG issues is a great place to start when digging into a brand's say/do gap. Of all the issues that are most important to the brand's operational realities and how it affects both the planet and society, how is the company doing?

One of the best places to start an examination is a brand's annual sustainability/ESG report. But not every company looking to articulate and operationalize its purpose has a sustainability department that has executed a materiality assessment, let alone written an annual report. Even if these documents don't exist formally, they are likely on the minds of many stakeholders. From leadership to customers, from partners and suppliers to employees, anyone associated with your brand has insight into how the company both does now, and could in the future, show up as a positive actor in the health of the planet or the stability of society. It just takes some smart questions and careful listening.

For many brands either just getting started or those who might be considered midsized, a disciplined look at their say/do gap is best determined through executive intake sessions and stakeholder interviews.

Executive Intake Sessions

Senior executives are more and more aware that being able to articulate the brands' corporate purpose and how the company is organizing its resources, innovation, social capital, and brand value in support of that purpose is now one of their top responsibilities. According to research conducted by Porter Novelli, 97 percent of senior executives believe that "having a defined and clear corporate identity, principles and purpose helps executives make better decisions for the organization" (Porter Novelli, 2021b).

These leaders are a key source for inspiration and practical insights into what the company can aspire to when it comes to purpose. In my experience working with CEOs and others in the C-suite, there is a growing sense of both permission and trepidation when it comes to articulation of a brand purpose. Many are seeking to leverage their influence. More than 93 percent believe that they have a duty as a business executive to use their platform and authority to influence social issues. During the discovery phase, executive intake sessions provide the best way to explore both issues and assets that executives are seeing as critical to the company.

In a project with an outdoor apparel company, we interviewed members of the board, C-suite and top executives across operations, HR, procurement, partnerships, philanthropy, retail, and compliance departments. We asked them the same questions we asked their employees, but dug a little deeper to gauge their ability and appetite for deploying resources, calibrating expectations, and diverting capital from existing priorities in support of a shared purpose.

Across the board, there was consistent interest in finding and committing to a shared vision for a better world. In this case, it centered on the awareness that many of them were waking up to regarding the stresses affecting their employees, suppliers, customers, and families after years of a global pandemic, racial injustices, and hate crimes. Each of them talked about how being outdoors helped them cope and how much they wanted everyone to have that experience. They were ready to reorient retail stores, in-store classes, HR policies, philanthropy initiatives, and marketing campaigns to drive support for the restorative powers of being outdoors.

It's important to note that while current CEOs and executives can bring personal passions and issues to the forefront of this exploration, a true purpose must outlive current teams and be relevant to both the legacy and the future of a brand. Purpose statements should outlive current executive teams because they express both a need in the commons and a unique approach that is true to a brand's essence.

Stakeholder Interviews

An important dimension of purpose exploration is a careful mapping of the stakeholder landscape whose opinions about a brand's purpose and legacy. These individuals and organizations can include both internal and external representatives who bring both inside knowledge of the company as well as an outside perspective. When we conduct these interviews, we are looking to uncover information about what the brand uniquely represents in how it participates in both environmental and social issues. What we are looking for is some of what is also in a materiality assessment—where do the assets of the company meet the needs of the world?

Stakeholders both inside and outside the company can help surface innovations, market realities, or operational hot spots that point to issues and opportunities worth exploring. For a food company, for example, exploration of material issues reveals that agriculture and transportation are two of the biggest impact areas when it comes to environmental impacts. Looking at solutions can reveal that regenerative agriculture practices—both at the soil and community level—are a rich place for purpose exploration. The concept of regeneration, deploying systems that constantly restore themselves for the good of every member in the system, can be expressed as an organizational purpose that philanthropy and manufacturing, procurement and innovation can orient themselves around.

Employee Focus Groups

Purpose exploration focus groups are an essential element in discovery because they give employees at every level and region in the company a chance to participate. Employees are the closest to the actual business of the business—whether on the manufacturing floor or in the warehouse, in research labs or retail stores. They tend to deal directly with the customers, and watch the products or services perform on the ground in real life. They grapple with resource constraints and the conflicting pressures of business KPIs. Because they make the choice every day to stay committed to a brand and its goals, they have a unique perspective of what the lived experience is at the company in a way the executives may be somewhat removed from. Mostly, employees can be your most honest critics when it comes to determining a brand's say/do gap.

Common questions we ask during the focus group are:

- Tell us about a time you were particularly proud of our company. Which of our values shined through?

- What words would you use to describe company culture? Why?

- What social issues are authentic to our brands?

- What impact do we hope to have in the world? How do our products play a part?

- What do you want us to be known for as a brand?
- If this company didn't exist, what would the world be missing?
- What do we wish people knew about our company that they don't know now?

One of the most important aspects of intake sessions, interviews, and focus groups is how these touchpoints create engagement across the organization. Defining and deploying a brand purpose takes buy-in along the process. For the outcome to be authentic, express the shared vision and heart of the brand, the upfront discovery process is designed to gain both insights and buy-in. When people are part of the process, they become advocates and leaders in operationalizing purpose across functions.

2. Customer Insights

Whether the brand is B2B or sells products and services to consumers, customers are an important stakeholder in the purpose process of every business. Some companies have extensive consumer insights departments that explore every aspect of what products people are looking for, what benefits they expect from those products, what price, features, or availability is needed to convert interest into purchase.

However, consumer insights and research about purchase intent can sometimes be devoid of insight into what people believe about the company making the product. Purpose and sustainability research since 2008 has been testing what people want from both the products they buy but also what they expect from the companies who make those products.

In the early days of sustainability and purpose, it was all about the product. How was it made? Was it a "green" product? In the last decade, we've seen consumers take a much closer look at the companies they buy from. They are looking for proof that the companies are responsible, take care of their employees, and are responsible stewards of the environment. It is now both a product-plus-company purchase calculation.

During discovery, explore what you know about your customers from primary research you may have conducted, or look among the myriad of research projects that are dissecting the "intention to action" gap among consumers when it comes to purchasing and behaving sustainably. Research from Porter Novelli that says Gen Z will do their homework to make sure a company lives up to its social commitments with actions that address racism or inequality. Sixty-four percent of Gen Z believe companies have a role to play in addressing social justice issues and 50 percent have done research to see what companies have done to make progress against the commitments they made to social justice issues (Porter Novelli, 2021a).

Whether from SB Brands for Good's (2022) socio-cultural trend tracker or the Collage Group's (2022) look at diverse consumer attitudes, the data is becoming consistent and compelling. Consumers of varying incomes, gender identity, race, ethnicity, or education levels are looking to brands to help them live more sustainable lives. This becomes the opening for a purposeful brand to offer a vision of how to help. We are seeing the shift from hero brands to enabler brands. Your purpose should answer this question: who can you help people become?

3. Competitive Analysis

Competitive analyses are straightforward exercises whenever brands want to understand how they stack up against their peer group. In purpose discovery, benchmarking goes a little deeper than just what companies are communicating to a closer look at their operational initiatives when it comes to environmental or social issues. In most cases, the answers can be found in their sustainability or ESG reports as well as an assessment of their marketing and communications campaigns, social feeds, and philanthropic initiatives.

The other dimension of a competitive analysis is to be focused on a tight set of companies who compete on a customer, market, and resources level. You do not want to include every company in your financial peer set but rather those that you routinely sell against or get compared to when consumers are price or feature shopping. The benefit of a small set for a competitor purpose benchmarking is to see where in the environmental or social issues arena others are offering a vision or perspective so that an open space for differentiation that is true to your brand can be explored. We are looking for that blue sky space that can be owned by your brand—one that is needed, is relevant, is not duplicative of other efforts and is authentic to your brand persona.

I've always said that there is much needed from businesses in protecting and preserving the commons. From clean air to fresh water, from protected species to access to healthcare or to the arts, companies don't need to elbow each other out of the way to do good. There is much to do and competing on purpose is not the answer. Better businesses will need to collaborate with each other to take a systems approach to climate change or social inequity. Differentiating on purpose is the goal. How does your unique vision for a greater good drive brand value, increase employee loyalty, create lasting partnerships? That's the space we want to explore with a smart competitive assessment.

Some common areas for exploration, rating and weighting in your analysis include mission and purpose statement, campaign and activations, sustainability and ESG goals and targets from greenhouse gas (GHG) emissions to renewable energy, from diversity and inclusion commitments to equality and justice programs, news coverage, social media campaigns, product portfolios and procurement or supplier commitments. What you're looking for are patterns across and between the companies that show trends within your industry.

For apparel companies, the biggest issues are the planetary harm caused by fast fashion and the toxicity inherent in the manufacturing process from dyes, glues, the intensive water use in cotton farming, and the legacy of exploitative labor practices in the supply chain. Inherent within these challenges are opportunities for purpose that tackle either the environmental or human dimension. And, many brands have begun to take these opportunities.

4. Cultural Tailwinds

This discovery dimension is a little art and a little science. It takes the mind of a cultural anthropologist and a spirit of curiosity. This is not research to determine what's trendy. It's not only looking at what's hot on TikTok or Twitter, but it should include a social media scan. It takes some discernment to sort out trends from trendy. To look at both macro socio-political movements, economic indicators, behavioral shifts, ethical norm adjustments.

There are a few places I go to suss out where the tailwinds and headwinds are shifting when it comes to attitudes and beliefs held by consumers and citizens. To see who is rising in influence and whose cultural capital is waning I scan Trendwatching.com and sparksandhoney.com. I read American Demographics, Five Thirty-Eight blog, and Rand.org. I scan *The Economist*, the *Financial Times*, the *Guardian* and Instagram. I look for the broad strokes of movements and zeitgeist within which a brand's purpose needs to find relevance and resonance. It is important not to be distracted by what's trending because purpose must be enduring and outlast the trendy. Trends, however, can point to what's emerging from a social construct perspective. They can reveal what commons are in jeopardy or might show early signs of either decay or growth.

Racial injustice is part of the historical fabric of the United States. Additionally, the systemic "othering" of religions, tribes, sects, or skin colors has always been present throughout human history. What we saw emerge in 2020 in the US following the murder of George Floyd and the expansion of the Black Lives Matter movement is now beginning to ripple around the world. It is a growing public discourse about all of the dimensions of diversity, inclusion, equity, and justice which has proven to be fertile ground for many brands' purpose.

Another trending issue is climate change, especially after the harsh realities laid bare following the global Covid-19 pandemic. "In modern industrial societies, the fallout from Covid-19 feels like a dress rehearsal for the kind of collapse that climate change threatens," said Jem Bendell, professor of sustainability leadership and founder of the Institute for Leadership and Sustainability at the University of Cumbria, in an interview. "This crisis reveals how fragile our current way of life has become." Bendell is well known among environmentalists for his theory of "deep adaptation." In a 2018 paper, Bendell said that time was up for gradual measures to combat global warming. Without an abrupt transformation of society, changes in the planet's climate would bring starvation, destruction, migration, disease, and war—and the collapse of civilization—within a decade (Bloomberg, 2020).

The cultural tailwinds which can propel purpose forward or the headwinds like the predictions of civilization collapse are critical components for brand purpose exploration. Companies must look squarely at the challenges ahead and not be tempted to dismiss them as hyperbole or mistake them for anything more than predictions. They must also be willing to have a dialogue about where and how the company can enter the challenge and contribute resources to a solution. It takes the imagination and sense of agency that companies have a right and a responsibility to participate in big issues.

The cultural exploration component of discovery is meant to be instructive and thematic, not prescriptive or a formal forecasting exercise. This is not risk assessment or trying to predict outcomes with any certainty. Rather, it is bringing external pressures and uplifts that can affect a business as it sets upon its purpose journey.

Blue Sky Ideation

The creation of a unique purpose statement that accurately and authentically represents a brand comes into shape following the synthesis of all that was revealed in the discovery phase. You start with what is true about the company—its legacy and founding story, its mission, vision, and values, where it is leaning into environmental or social issues and where it is coming up short against its own goals and commitments.

You compare all of that with peers to see where the gaps are between and among other companies in the sector. Given the shared challenges and opportunities to build both customer engagement and employee loyalty, who is doing something unique and interesting as a response to the needs of the greater good? And where is there space for a different or new approach?

A useful tool for ideating a purpose statement is a two-by-two (2x2) quadrant that positions competitors along a horizontal and vertical axis. For each company, industry, and competitive set, the two vectors may change. One pairing might be between topic and tone. Another might be limited involvement versus activist activities. Or perhaps being a solo leader versus bringing others along. What a

2x2 competitive quadrant gives you is a clear way to place your brand along with those in your peer set and find the blue-sky space that you already occupy that is different from your peers. Once that space is identified, then the work comes in articulating your response to the opportunity in a way that is true to your brand personality. One that can be expressed in a manifesto that includes the components of a master narrative—what we believe, the change we want to see in the world, the barriers to that change and what we will do about them, and, lastly, a vision for the future.

Once the blue sky territory has been mapped, and a manifesto written that expresses the fullness of your purpose ambition, it is important to present the new but not-finalized approach via a workshop to again ensure buy-in from key stakeholders. Creating a purpose manifesto from synthesized research requires stakeholder reactions and push back. For it to hold up over time, it requires rigorous interrogation of the commitment it implies.

Once key stakeholders have weighed in and helped refine, you have a finished purpose statement that can be operationalized across every department, used to engage every stakeholder group, and leveraged to drive brand value. The exercise of defining purpose gives marketing and sales a way to help win customers and enhance their loyalty. For HR, it can attract, engage, and retain employees. For governance and sustainability, it can enhance environmental, social, and governance performance. For strategy and finance, it can guide how resources are allocated and risks are managed. And for innovation and R&D, it can unlock creativity because it focuses and refines not only what you are making, but who you are making it for. It gives you permission to explore new territories and approaches that link products and services to generating greater good.

Plan Development

The exercise of defining purpose gives marketing and sales a way to help win customers and enhance their loyalty. For HR, it can attract, engage, and retain employees. For governance and sustainability, it can enhance environmental, social, and governance performance. For strategy and finance, it can guide how resources are allocated and risks are managed. And for innovation and R&D, it can unlock creativity because it focuses and refines not only what you are making, but who you are making it for. It gives you permission to explore new territories and approaches that link products and services to generating greater good.

Once the purpose statement and manifesto are approved, the hard task of change management begins. Initially, a purpose plan has two critical components. The first is a prioritization of the departments and process that will be most directly impacted by the purpose. An initial task force of key stakeholders is needed to begin operationalizing the purpose strategy. There should also be the formation of some type of governance structure to ensure the company delivers on its vision, sets clear goals, deploys resources, and tracks progress for ongoing reporting.

The second important element of a purpose plan is a comprehensive communications plan that includes a launch strategy. A launch moment which debuts a call to action for all employees is the first step in the type of organizational change needed for a company to authentically live out its purpose.

CASE STUDY   Abercrombie & Fitch

In 2019, with new CEO Fran Horowitz in place, Abercrombie & Fitch Company (A&F Co.) was shedding its "bad boy" image of the past, moving from mean, cliquey, and exclusive to passionately inclusive and decidedly customer-centric. From its focus on expanding and improving as an omni-channel retailer with frictionless purchase experiences either in store or online, A&F Co. was looking to re-engage with the customers from its early years, who experienced the brand as teenagers, who were now parents of young teenagers themselves.

Under Fran's leadership, A&F Co.'s brands were exploring purpose at the individual brand level and looking to both harmonize a shared purpose across its brands (A&F, A&F Kids, Hollister, and Gilly Hicks) while laddering a sense of shared intention at the enterprise level.

A&F Co.'s brands were developing gender neutral clothing, demonstrating commitment to size inclusivity, employing diverse models and spokespeople, and engaging in courageous conversations about diversity, equity, and inclusion. Under Fran's leadership, the enterprise was establishing a track record on supporting LGBTQ+ and women in the workforce and wanted to create an enterprise-wide purpose agenda for the organizations that could be a red thread through operational as well as philanthropic efforts. A&F brought in Porter Novelli to explore, refine and articulate the company's purpose.

Assessing the landscape was a key part of the process, including a close look at the competitive set—how they are positioning themselves, the nature of their impact and commitments in order to find differentiated territory that was unique to A&F Co.

We synthesized our findings from the landscape assessment and deskside research into an initial direction plotted on a 2x2. The horizontal X axis was defined as Corporate Action vs. Consumer Empowerment. The vertical or Y-axis was Individual Progress versus Social Good. What we discovered was that most companies were in the Social Good approach to purpose initiatives, leading with their own corporate activities. The blue sky space was in a brand that helped its customers reach their own potential as fully empowered people. This spoke to the strong commitment A&F Co. had already been leaning into when it came to DEI across gender, race, ethnicity, and size inclusivity.

A&F Co. is a consensus-driven organization that prides itself on having a culture that makes space for input at all levels of the company. During the purpose development process, we collaborated with people across the globe and from all corners of the company via interviews, surveys, focus groups, and consumer research projects.

The insights gathered from the employee listening sessions had a significant impact on the final purpose strategy. The first was that many consumers know the portfolio of brands are connected to each other and give them credit for playing an important role in their lives throughout the most formative years. This was something that we learned from in store associates who were closest to the customers. And it was confirmed by the Gen Z Sounding Boards, A&F Co.'s newest employees who grew up shopping the brands from A&F Kids, to Hollister and then A&F.

The second insight that emerged was a frustration that existed across the organization about their inability to shed their "mean girl" image from the past no matter how much the company had changed from the days of its previous and infamous CEO Mike Jeffries and his exclusionary approach to the company (MacKelden, 2022). People wanted the company to be known for who they were today.

Where we landed after all of the feedback and synthesis was an enterprise purpose statement that had individualized relevance to each brand, captured the essence of the organization's heart and intention, and gave employees a unifying sense of why they exist as a fashion brand.

One deeply moving experience with the Abercrombie & Fitch project came during an early intake session at the company's headquarters campus in Columbus, Ohio. It's a beautiful bucolic setting, rolling hills with small sunlight grass fields set amid wooded forests, the buildings nestled in a forest, looking more like modern outdoorsy lodging than a corporate headquarters facility. One of the main features on campus is a massive outdoor fireplace surrounded by chairs and benches. This is where Fran usually hosts her quarterly all hands meetings which are also beamed to locations all around the world. Dubbed Gather Round, these assemblies give associates a chance to hear more about the status of the business, ask questions of leaders, and hear progress on community initiatives.

That first campus tour and two days of meetings included sessions with Fran and her executive team. It also involved separate meetings with leadership from each of the four brands and their creative teams—both the designers and marketers who were responsible for what was created for each line as well as those responsible for in-store experience as well as all advertising.

I remember the conversation as free-flowing and energizing. What struck me the most from both the A&F team and the Hollister team—many of whom had relocated from New York or Los Angeles fashion companies to this Midwest campus—was how seriously they took their responsibility as culture shapers. They knew who A&F was in the lives of adolescents and young adults and understood how powerful fashion and pop culture are in including, accepting, and making space for all identities. As we explored what purpose meant to them and how they saw their role as designers and creatives, they allowed their imaginations to envision a world where everyone felt seen and empowered on their journey from childhood to adulthood. They talked about how they were creating safe spaces for those in the LGBTQ+ space both in front and behind the camera of photo-shoots. They talked about clothing as a palette of expression that they wanted to make as inviting and inclusive as possible.

I left my time in Columbus with a truth I often experience in my work. That businesses and brands are full of good people who feel deeply their responsibility to the commons. That they understand how they uniquely can use their job, their decisions, their influence to create positive change in the world.

References

Abercrombie & Fitch (2022) Press releases, Abercrombie & Fitch, https://corporate.abercrombie.com/investors/newsevents/press-releases (archived at https://perma.cc/X93F-VQLG)

Aziz, A (2019) The power of purpose: How Procter & Gamble is becoming "a force for good and a force for growth" pt1, Forbes, www.forbes.com/sites/afdhelaziz/2019/07/16/the-power-of-purpose-how-procter-and-gamble-is-becoming-a-force-for-good-a-force-for-growth-pt1 (archived at https://perma.cc/J7BQ-GB3B)

Bloomberg (2020) Professor sees climate mayhem lurking behind covid-19 Outbreak, Bloomberg Law, https://news.bloomberglaw.com/coronavirus/professor-sees-climate-mayhem-lurking-behind-covid-19-outbreak (archived at https://perma.cc/S94J-2NAQ)

Collage Group (2022) Multicultural market research, Collage Group, www.collagegroup.com/audiences/multicultural/multicultural-market-research/5 (archived at https://perma.cc/UAX8-4Q9A)

eBay (2022) September 1995: AuctionWeb is born, eBay Inc, www.ebayinc.com/company/our-history (archived at https://perma.cc/RF7B-QK84)

Global Reporting (2021) Disclosure 3-3 in GRI3, Global Reporting, https://globalreporting.org/publications/documents/english/gri-3-material-topics-2021 (archived at https://perma.cc/F6J2-TVJZ)

Jones, B (2016) The difference between purpose and mission, Sponsored content from Disney Institute, *Harvard Business Review*, https://hbr.org/sponsored/2016/02/the-difference-between-purpose-and-mission (archived at https://perma.cc/WYW2-JHY7)

MacKelden, A (2022) Netflix's *White Hot* explores Mike Jeffries' complicated history with Abercrombie & Fitch, Harpers Bazaar, www.harpersbazaar.com/culture/film-tv/a39736086/who-is-mike-jeffries-abercrombie-and-fitch-netflix-white-hot (archived at https://perma.cc/2CTX-RA7E)

Porter Novelli (2021a) 2021 Porter Novelli focus: Gen Z and justice, PN, www.porternovelli.com/findings/2021-porter-novelli-focus-gen-z-justice (archived at https://perma.cc/Z4HL-J2KW)

Porter Novelli (2021b) The 2021 Porter Novelli executive influence study, PN, www.porternovelli.com/findings/the-2021-porter-novelli-executive-influence-study (archived at https://perma.cc/K9CE-TZFD)

SB Brands for Good (2022) Socio-cultural trends, SB Brands for Good, https://sbbrandsforgood.com/socio-cultural-trends (archived at https:// perma.cc/J5Q4-R68H)

Securities and Exchange Commission (1999) SEC staff accounting bulletin: No. 99 – materiality, www.sec.gov/interps/account/sab99.htm (archived at https://perma.cc/L53S-SW37)

Operationalizing Sustainability/ ESG Across Silos 03

From Purpose to Sustainability, Operationalizing in ESG Rigor

Purpose is a poetic expression of the greater good that a company will create in the world, using its business as a mechanism for delivering a regenerative planet and an equitable society. Exploring what, how, where, and for whom a company makes its products or services reveals ethical imperatives that corporations need to consider. They are also entry points into sustainability strategy and ESG programs.

Purpose is all about a vision for protecting, nurturing, or restoring the commons. Purpose is not sustainability. It is not ESG. Conflating these terms into one amorphous blob of overlapping meaning is not helpful. Let's break down what each of these are, how they are inter-related and why sustainability and ESG are effective dimensions that can help any brand deliver the promise inherent in its purpose.

There are any number of articles and books that tell businesses to use their purpose to guide their core strategy. So do I. Purpose is the North Star for your entire business—when you get it right, it breaks open creativity and innovation around products, services, and markets. When it comes to sustainability, focusing on purpose alone risks ignoring critical ESG commitments that fall outside a company's purpose.

Let's look at the example of A&F Co. Their North Star, their purpose is "We are here for you on the journey to being and becoming who you are." For A&F, it orients the company, its designers and creators, its HR and talent teams, its marketing and communications departments, its community, and philanthropic efforts to building a welcoming and celebratory business that advocates and protects all identities. But does this mean they can ignore their environmental impacts? Not at all. While their purpose does not explicitly include the environmental aspects of the fashion industry as many others do—Patagonia, Eileen Fisher, Everlane—A&F Co. has a robust sustainability department that is working hard to reduce the company's GHG emissions and waste.

And, A&F Co.'s DEI initiatives, which are part of their social sustainability strategy, are a big component of how they live out their purpose. The way that the HR department recruits, retains, promotes, and celebrates a diverse workforce is an operational expression of their purpose. So is the way in which they prioritize the human dimension of their supply chain. They can extend "becoming who you are" in training programs that support women leaders in a diverse supplier network. In the case of A&F Co., their purpose is weighted in the social dimension but in no way diminishes the company's commitment to its environmental efforts.

When we expect organizations to do "all things sustainability," we risk scattering their attention and diluting progress on their purpose, let alone business performance. We also risk deprioritizing or

Figure 3.1   Purpose–sustainability–ESG

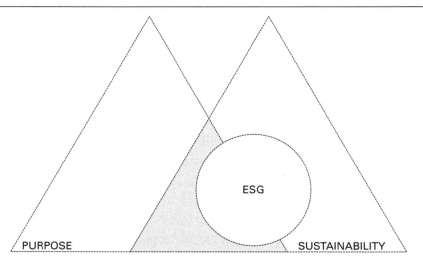

ignoring the many dimensions of sustainability that are essential to every brand. In many ways, sustainability and ESG are now table stakes for any well-run responsible company.

So, what is sustainability? First, it has always been both the environmental and social dimensions of a business. Sustainability, which is a strategic approach, is one element to operationalizing purpose across the entire value chain—all the way up the supply chain even to materials sourcing, processing, and contract manufacturing and then, all the way down to end-of-life and how customers use your product.

When a brand gets its sustainability strategy right, it will be one of the ways it delivers on brand purpose. ESG is the environment, social, and governance mechanism by which an organization tracks, measures, and reports on how it is doing against its sustainability strategy. ESG without sustainability strategy becomes just a target, a thing, a box to check. Sustainability without purpose can miss the underlying brand essence and brand value that makes a company and what it does unique and differentiable from its peers.

Purpose unlocks creativity, giving a brand permission to create products, markets and, customers that it never thought of before. It should also give the company permission to say no to the thing that takes it off strategy, sends it on some random goose chase, or encourages it to react to market pressures or anomalies. Purpose is the singular organizing construct that gives you a sense of direction to every decision you make as a business.

Integrated Communications

Porter Novelli research that we deployed consistently during 2020 through 2022, along with many other studies from a range of other organizations, shows over and over that people want to know that they are buying a good product from a company that's good. I use the word "good" as a placeholder for a company that's paying attention to all the things that sit within purpose and sustainability. But all those stakeholders need to hear more about what the company is pledging, how they are making progress.

The best way to move into operationalizing purpose is to create a specific sustainability platform, which has that rallying cry for what the brand is uniquely delivering from an environmental and social perspective. Underneath are pillars that frame a company's ambition and how they will deliver progress against goals. These take shape as climate commitments, net-zero commitments, commitments to divest of oil and gas, or DEI programs and progress. From there a brand needs to create the narrative, the messaging, the proof points, the press releases, and then all the communications assets that are deployed across the owned, earned, and paid channels. Internal and external communications are essential components from the very beginning when a brand sets its purpose, creates a sustainability strategy, and then operationalizes it through ESG programs.

Why is communication essential? Because behavior change is, at its core, storytelling. How do you get everyone on board, engaged, and rowing in the same direction? Whether you have 10 or 100,000 employees, narratives, messages, examples, and campaigns matter.

From my perspective in corporate communications for more than 30 years, I believe that public relations professionals are the organizational anthropologists and cultural watchers needed to synthesize external insights with internal truths. This is especially true when it comes to the shifting realities of climate change and social equity. We already deal with the communications to every stakeholder; that is classic PR. We are constantly watching what's happening out in culture so that we can better communicate. What has changed is the information that we are now responsible for—it goes beyond corporate communications and product information. We will take a deep dive into communications' role in purpose and sustainability as well as a close look at the techniques and principles of accurate and differentiated storytelling in Chapter 9.

Business and capitalism are changing, and we need new stories, new frameworks, and new ambitions. It is helpful to pay attention to the ways in which expectations and norms are shifting. It is happening all around, easy to miss. There are more and more writers, trend watchers, economists, and demographers questioning so many of the business and value assumptions that have organized brands for decades.

Following the launch of David Gelles' 2022 book *The Man Who Broke Capitalism*, he was interviewed by one of the best new thinkers on wealth and capitalism, Anand Giridharadas. In that conversation, he asked Gelles a pointed question about purpose, business, and the role of capitalism, "Have you seen any evidence that the pledge resulted in businesses behaving differently, workers being treated differently, and taxes being paid differently? Did that shift cause anything, or was it window dressing?" (Giridharadas, 2022).

Gelles' answer tied back to his coverage of Business Roundtable's pronouncement about stakeholder capitalism in 2019. He confirmed what many others have said, that despite this public statement—made a few months before the pandemic hit—about caring for all stakeholders, CEOs led massive layoffs and, in many cases, abandoned their employees when they needed support the most. But Gelles also said something else that mirrors my experience.

What Gelles describes as a reporter who has been reporting on trends within the business sector is a palpable shift in how businesses, and specifically CEOs, see their role in society. Certainly, there is skepticism that this shift is authentic, but as he sees it—and so do I—leaders are coming to terms with the reality that to retain talent or ensure resiliency in the face of extreme weather, dealing explicitly with climate change is a business imperative. The decades-long pendulum shift away from Welchism is fully underway and CEOs are being asked, by employees, customers, communities, and even investors to demonstrate responsibility for more than just expected profits:

> What's good for business is a healthy, sustainable economy where a growing number of people have the means to buy goods and services. That doesn't happen when the minimum wage stays stuck at $7.25. It should be close to $25 if it had just kept pace with inflation over the last 25 years. So "good for business" is not good for business as we know it. It's good for a more sustainable kind of business that would be acceptable for all of us.
>
> (Giridharadas, 2022)

Brand Transformation

Since 2007, I have been a member of the Sustainable Brands community, attending the annual conference, participating as a speaker or panelist, serving on the Advisory Board as a lifetime appointee. Over the last 15 years, I have honed my technical skills, built a network of practitioners who I can call on to collaborate or advise, and leveraged the tools built to help companies on their sustainability journey.

One asset that has been invaluable to over two hundred organizations is the SB Brand Transformation Roadmap (SM). This is an orientation and navigation tool that maps out the entire sustainability journey and allows a company to assess the maturity of its efforts in five critical practice areas: purpose, brand influence, operations and supply chain, products and services, and governance.

The way in which this tool lays out the interrelationships between purpose and the operational dimensions where sustainability strategy and implementation take place gives every company the framework needed to assess and advance. The fact that each of these five dimensions has five levels, from "conventional" to "sustainable brand", illuminates how companies can be ahead in some areas and move more slowly in others. The most important takeaway is that a company needs to be executing across all five dimensions with at least a conventional or table stakes effort.

I have developed a similar maturity model that I use to help executives assess both where they believe themselves to be and where they want to go. Such a model provides a way for companies to see where resources may already be deployed, where they are needed and where advancement serves the business most effectively and where a functional or baseline effort is enough.

Purpose and Sustainability Leadership Continuum

The challenge with developing a sustainability strategy to deliver on purpose is that there are effectively hundreds of elements within each of the five practice areas identified by the SB Brand Transformation

Figure 3.2 Continuum from compliance to leadership applies to every operational element and issue

	COMPLIANCE	PROGRAMMATIC	STRATEGIC	LEADERSHIP
MOTIVATION	Minimum legal requirement	Some risk avoidance	Business advantage	Generating societal value that benefits all
STRATEGIC INTENT	Reduction in friction	Departmental success	Business value	Humanity's success through shared value
STRUCTURE	Regulatory	Siloed	Connection to brand and products	North Star
RESOURCES	Minimal	Departmental	Cross-functional	Full integration
TRANSPARENCY	Legally minimal	Episodic	Annual and integrated	On-going communications with all stakeholders
POSITION	Reactive	Follower	Industry sector leadership	Proactive multi-dimensional leadership

Roadmap. And then there is the progress you might be making against any one of those hundreds of elements. It is helpful to take a closer look at the dimensions along the continuum of sustainability leadership (Figure 3.2) and recognize that no brand can be a leader in all dimensions. In some cases, a brand's decision might be to be a follower, or simply be compliant in an operational capacity so that capital resources can be deployed more freely in another.

Contemplating the Big Questions

I've used this continuum as an assessment tool with C-suite executives, asking each of them to place their company along each of the elements for a wide range of issues or commitments. In every case, there needs to be a clear-eyed view of the resources, ambitions, or barriers to progress that confront a brand when determining how it will show up and what its ambitions are. We usually start with a single question or issue area: climate change, DEI, pay equity. But this tool can be used across any material issue.

Following the completion of a materiality assessment, a company will have a list of the elements and issues that are the most directly relevant to both the company's success as well as the environmental and social dimensions within which that company operates. That is the first step in helping a brand orient how to set sustainability goals and programs. Then comes the question—but how big do we want to go? How strongly do we want to lead? Can we lead? Should we? There are a few right answers to those questions and many more that are a leadership team's collective assessment of ambition, legacy, along with stakeholders' views, are the most important to the brand's future. Sometimes, it comes down to an executive team's personal sense of "It's just the right thing to do." These questions will keep coming up again and again for any company that expects to survive the next 50 years and the massive shifts that are happening everywhere.

Alex Steffen has created a new worldview that he describes in his newsletter, podcast and book called *The Snap Forward*. A climate futurist and former business journalist, Steffen beautifully articulates the place we are in and the ways in which all of us, brands included, must accept the scope and scale of change that is already with us and will be required of us (Steffen, 2022).

Let's start with a look at what he means by a worldview. A worldview is a set of beliefs or a mental model of reality that influences the way people perceive, think, know, and act in the world. I understand what he is talking about so clearly. This is what I try to say in my TEDx talk about the power of "Yes—and" (Skees, 2019). About how becoming marginalized when I came out forced a change in my worldview. I suddenly saw hypocrisy, homophobia, those who were "in" and those who were "out." I am painfully aware of how many Black, Asian, Indigenous, and religiously persecuted people have known these truths from their earliest memories. I know that my privilege as a white cis woman born in the US insulated me from a worldview that included discrimination and harm. The ability to see both realities is nonbinary thinking and is what Steffen is getting at.

In his book Steffen talks about how all of us have grown up in societies that view the world in a particular way, causing us to hold assumptions about how the world should work. However, many of us have since come to understand how those assumptions and worldviews were wrong in a myriad of ways. He discusses how in just one human's lifetime we have done so much damage to our planet, altering the climate and biosphere and destabilizing core systems that we rely on to survive. His assertion that our lives are discontinuous with those that came before us, and that we now live in societies unsuited for the world we've created, hit home for me—the reminder that, even though we all are now seeing the catastrophic change all around, we still often view the planet with those same perspective we formed as part of our societal worldview.

What happens, according to Steffen's theory, is that once a new reality is in place, like a warmed planet that is already experiencing species loss and extreme weather, people will either be forced to see this new reality or expend a tremendous amount of energy denying its existence. We have certainly seen that play out over the last two decades.

When he turns to the question of climate change, his words get starker, discussing how the rate of change is faster than we are able to truly understand and likening this rate of change to a storm that's out at sea but whilst the sky is dark and the sea is choppy, the storm is not yet in our view.

When I think about the times my wife and I have been out on the Monterey Bay in our sailboat, keeping an eye on the weather, that last sentence resonates viscerally. It's scary when you feel the power of winds, choppy waters, and big swells, and see dark clouds not far off. You calculate how much time you have to get the boat safely back at the dock before the storm actually hits. You drop your sails, turn on the engine and accelerate as fast as you can to get ahead of the worsening weather.

So, it is no small thing to accept the truth Steffen describes when it comes to the rate of change and how our current worldview needs to change very quickly so we can navigate the storm. Steffen refers to this moment of recognition as "the snap forward," that is, "the sudden recalibration of assumptions, plans and priorities in the face of the truth of our moment." He claims that it is this moment of recognition that forces us to accept that our worldviews no longer make sense in our realities and see that actually:

> We live in a time of discontinuous realities and the loss of predictable outcomes; of new needs and disruptive solutions; of transapocalyptic tragedies and fierce political fights to increase the pace of action; of looming failures of systemic value… and scales of opportunity with no historical analogue.
>
> (Steffen, 2022)

Whew. That is a lot to take in. But it's an important place to stand when asking the right questions about where and how a brand is going to lean into purpose and use sustainability to set a course for getting where they need to go. Companies who do not understand the reality of the moment, who will not look squarely at what needs to change and how fast, may not live the 50-plus years that their purpose statement should endure.

Continuum Elements

During this era of change and discontinuity, the continuum tool becomes a way to initially and then periodically assess how a brand looks at each of its prioritized material topics and determine how they will respond to the challenge ahead. No one can lead at every-thing, but everyone must lead at something.

Motivation

What is under consideration here is the intention and motivation ap-plied against the challenge. Using GHG or carbon emissions as an example, the motivation can start with simply meeting the minimum legal requirements and ensuring regulatory compliance with air qual-ity standards at manufacturing facilities. As regulatory bodies around the globe continue to look more closely at GHG emissions, we can expect that minimum legal requirements will increase beyond not polluting. But motivation can move up the spectrum to program-matic and the design for some risk avoidance that goes a bit beyond regulatory compliance. Many companies are in this phase now as they contemplate the risks associated with the effects of climate change—the weather disruptions and supply change anomalies.

Dual materiality and risk management disciplines explore both the impact a company's operations are having on the environment, and the effect that climate change is having on the company. Having pro-grammatic motivation, in the case of GHG, is to understand the dual risk profile and want to create programs that address it.

Strategic motivation sees a sustainability issue as an opportunity to gain a business advantage. The carbon intensity that data center companies experience when powering acres of high-speed servers is an example of carbon reduction as a business advantage. The rising cost of energy as well as the carbon footprint of fossil fuel powered electricity has motivated many technology companies like Google, Amazon, and Iron Mountain to deploy renewable energy installa-tions across their data center networks and supplant with renewable energy purchase agreements for the remainder of their energy needs. The business advantage is in reduced energy costs and the reduction of an overall carbon footprint.

Motivated leaders seek change that creates business advantage but, beyond that, creates values that extend not only to their sector but to the world at large. There are few examples of sustainability leadership but more and more are emerging as executives realize that, in order to achieve a singular business advantage, an entire system will need to change. Truly, a rising tide will raise all boats.

Strategic Intent

The four stages of strategic intent have similar dimensions as motivation. But where motivation represents a brand's interaction with external groups (regulators, collaborators, systems), strategic intent is faced inward.

Compliance intent is simply to reduce operational friction, to make sure that laws are followed, and fines or stoppages avoided. Let's use supplier programs as an example for strategic intent. In the compliance phase, managing vendor relations and a compliance program is a great strategy for reducing costs, speeding up order processing, and reducing warehousing and freight costs. Meeting those baseline business requirements is the objective of a compliance sustainability program. The environmental or social dimensions within the supplier network are not considered beyond legal requirements.

Programmatic intent looks at only departmental success. The environmental or social dimensions are considered and sought because they deliver value to the specific department rather than the enterprise as a whole. This level is exemplified by siloed departments each seeking sustainability advance that is limited to the parameters of what is controllable within the department itself.

Strategic intent looks for broader business value, beyond a departmental benefit. When a brand takes a position or sets a public goal pertaining to an environmental or social issue, like zero waste to landfill or diversity in leadership positions, they are expressing a belief that achieving those goals will drive value to the business overall. These brands are looking for progress in a particular issue to generate layers of business value.

Leadership intent expresses a brand's willingness to leverage what it has learned from its own struggles and accomplishments within a material issue and share its learnings to lead both within and outside its sector in driving universal change.

An example of both the strategic and leadership levels is Starbucks' efforts in supporting coffee farmers and its role in the creation of Fairtrade designations. Starbucks buys approximately 3 percent of the world's coffee, sourced from more than 400,000 farmers in 30 countries. From its inception, Starbucks understood that its future is inextricably tied to the future of farmers and their families. They needed a reliable source of specialty coffee beans during the era when the coffee sector was dominated by large global brands like Maxwell House, Nescafé and Folgers. Starbucks needed a way to ensure they could dependably purchase the specially grown beans that were at the heart of their brand promise. These unique beans were typically the product of small growers and cooperatives whose livelihoods were dependent upon the middle layer of buyers and aggregators on behalf of the dominant buyer brands.

Starbucks has been working with Fairtrade globally since 2000. The main purpose of the Fairtrade movement is to provide an appropriate price to small-scale coffee farmers in developing countries to improve their lives. Beyond purchases on Fairtrade terms, Starbucks has funded more than $14 million in farmer loans to Fairtrade cooperatives as part of an ongoing commitment to helping farmers to manage risk and strengthen their businesses. Starbucks was the first private enterprise to invest in the Fairtrade Access Fund in 2012.

Another ethical sourcing approach to buying coffee is Starbuck's proprietary Coffee and Farmer Equity (C.A.F.E.) Practices, which was one of the coffee industry's first set of ethical sourcing standards when it launched in 2004. Developed in collaboration with Conservation International, C.A.F.E. Practices is a verification program that measures farms against economic, social, and environmental criteria, all designed to promote transparent, profitable, and sustainable coffee growing practices while also protecting the well-being of coffee farmers and workers, their families and their communities. C.A.F.E. Practices has helped Starbucks create a long-term supply of high-quality coffee and positively impact the lives and livelihoods of coffee farmers and their communities (Starbucks, 2022).

Structure

An important element of the continuum looks at how integrated the sustainability strategy is with the heart of the brand and its core operational aspects. This can range from the governance structure in place to guide and provide resources to the initiative, to the ways in which commitments and intent are woven into the products, innovation, and strategy for the company.

A compliance effort will deploy a regulatory framework that ensures laws are met. Usually exemplified by adherence to management systems like ISO, the International Organization for Standardization located in Geneva, Switzerland. ISO promotes the development and implementation of voluntary international standards, both for specific products and for environmental management issues. ISO 14001 is an internationally agreed standard that sets out the requirements for an environmental management system and one I came to know well during my years working at the British Standards Institute (BSI) in their US environment, health, safety (EHS) consulting group. The plan-do-check-act (PDCA) cycle is the operating model of all ISO management system standards, providing companies with a platform from which they can achieve continuous improvement.

Like other certification schemes, companies can choose simply to adhere to the standards without going through the effort and cost of obtaining certification. Brands at the far left of the continuum will likely seek guidance from the various aspects of standards like ISO 14001. This requires that an organization considers all environmental issues relevant to its operations, such as air pollution, water and sewage issues, waste management, soil contamination, climate change mitigation and adaptation, and resource use and efficiency.

Brands taking a programmatic approach to structure will develop a siloed approach to governance, tracking, and reporting of sustainability progress. Each department will set isolated goals, programs, metrics, and approaches that tackle issues relevant to its needs. Waste management is a good example. Any apparel manufacturer will need to manage the hazardous materials, mostly chemicals, that it uses when dying its products. Chemical dyes take a toll.

They can include compounds dangerous to the health of workers, ranging from chlorine bleach to known carcinogens such as arylamines. And if they aren't treated properly, they can pollute the water supply.

A programmatic approach will look only at the laws governing each chemical within each product line or department, rather than looking across the entire company or within multiple brand portfolios.

The strategic approach will look at value to a line of products or brands. In fact, most of the largest companies take a portfolio approach to solving environmental issues because of the inherent complexity of driving change across multiple brand portfolios. Strategic leadership in a global apparel company will see that the systems approach is best brand-by-brand rather than the more difficult effort of deploying across the needs of denim, shoes, athletic wear, and more.

Leaders see an environmental or social issue as their North Star. Their purpose is inextricably linked to their sustainability vision; and all the company's governance, resources, and brand identify are connected to the greater good they are creating for everyone. Patagonia is such a leader. While they have not solved every problem, they are tackling their environmental impacts across all dimensions of their business, from how they make their clothes and hard goods, to efforts at repair and recirculation. They are looking for solutions across the agricultural systems that provide cotton or goose down for their clothes to raw materials for their newly debuted provisions food line.

Resources

Resources are the capital expenditures, annual budgets, and staffing allocations that support meeting ESG commitments. They also include mindshare and what I call airtime—the places and conversations where the purpose programs and sustainability initiatives are talked about within the organization. Are updates provided internally on a regular basis? Are progress announcements made on owned, earned, and paid channels? Does the CEO regularly mention and acknowledge individuals and progress during quarterly updates?

Airtime acknowledges how much the purpose agenda has become part of the vernacular of business within the business.

Minimal is just that, scant resources deployed in support of any efforts that go beyond profitability at all cost. Any expense, whether it's someone's time or an actual cost associated with environmental or social betterment, is deemed unnecessary. Yet, even within the compliant category, there are always individuals who are trying to make a difference regardless of whether they receive additional resources or not. I have experienced over and over the delightful discovery of managers, hourly workers or mid-level executives who have been quietly going about making decisions that balance the needs of the company with those of the commons.

On one occasion, we were brought in by a newly appointed sustainability manager who had been given the daunting task of producing the semiconductor company's first ESG report. The position as well as the need for a report was in response to the growing interest from investment companies who held shares in the company that wanted a better understanding of how well the company was managing its environmental and social impacts. No one had ever looked across the company to determine its footprint, set a baseline, nor put any progress goals in place.

However, as we dug into our discovery phase and conducted stakeholder interviews, we learned in one manufacturing location renewable energy had been purchased because the ability to lock in purchase prices had penciled out to be a long-term cost saving. The initiative had gone unheralded, or was not seen as a sustainability win, because it had been done primarily to stabilize energy costs. But the facilities manager who pushed for the renewable energy purchase knew what the planetary benefits were. He just didn't call any attention to it. We uncovered several other examples of decisions like those that could eventually serve as the skeleton of a baseline ESG program for the report. What was missing was a top-down commitment and allocation of resources. But that was longer in coming from a company that continued to allocate only minimal resources to sustainability and part of another story.

Departmental resource allocation is the most common response to companies in the programmatic phase. These brands have selected a particular issue, like GHG or diversity in leadership, and are deploying time and resources at only the departmental level. It might be that diversity recruiting is supported only for entry-level positions in just one or two areas of the company. Or emissions are being studied and reduced at the manufacturing locations but not across all of the transportation levels when it comes to shipping and distribution of goods in and out of the company.

Strategic companies look at resource allocation across cross-functional departments, taking learnings from one process and applying them to adjacent challenges. A good example of this is in packaging advances. Many food producers are chasing 100 percent recycling packaging targets across their brands. This can be daunting as every food product has different needs when it comes to protecting the freshness and efficacy of the item. Snack bars are different from frozen bacon. But innovation departments are working with packaging and film companies to share information about the usefulness of various coatings and film characteristics. Working with suppliers and R&D departments, within food group clusters, strategic companies are working to solve recycling challenges across like brands.

Leaders adopt a full integration of the challenge across every category and product and find ways to drive organizational and cultural leadership. The "Every Bottle Back" initiative was launched by The Coca-Cola Company, Keurig, Dr Pepper and PepsiCo in an effort to reduce the industry's use of new plastic by making significant investments to improve the collection of the industry's valuable plastic bottles so they can be made into new bottles. What all three of these companies realized when attempting to meet ambitious recycling targets as well as their commitment to using post-consumer plastic (PCP) in new bottles is that the recycling rate of plastic bottles was abysmal (Recycling Partnership, 2022).

This industry initiative is a great example of the tension between the operational and cultural aspects of sustainability. It's why I have been a long-term supporter and leader within Sustainable Brands. We realize that we can't move our brands forward unless we bring culture along with us. What the leaders at The Coca-Cola Company, Keurig Dr Pepper and PepsiCo understand is the need to both increase recycling rates and work with the fragmented municipal recycling facilities to improve the PCP supply chain. These leaders have allocated significant resources to solving that missing link in their strategy and they are collaborating to achieve a common good—ecosystems devoid of plastic. This is just one way for the producers to take responsibility for the waste problem. There are many others under consideration by these three companies, including bulk packaging or even in home dispensers to reduce single use beverage consumption. It will take innovation across all dimensions and leaders to deploy resources to keep advancing.

Transparency

Along the continuum, how a brand communicates about its commitments, goals, progress, and challenges is a critical component of purpose and sustainability initiatives. We look at the content itself but also the frequency with which it tells the story and who is receiving the information. Both the message and messenger matter too. Is information shared by subject matter experts and senior leaders? Do advocates or partners participate and help validate?

Those in the compliance segment will offer only legally minimal information, providing only the data required and, in the format, expected. Information can only be found through much digging within disclosure documents like 10-K filings or in US EEO-1 (equal employment opportunity) submissions which may or may not have been made publicly available. These brands do not include environmental or social program information on their websites, do not publish an annual ESG or sustainability report, and have no interest in adding environmental messages to product labels or in-store signage.

Programmatic brands will provide information about goals episodically. These updates usually take the form of press releases announcing goals or participation in coalitions. There are rarely ongoing updates about progress but can be occasional social media posts with anecdotes about events or installations within a program.

Early in this sustainability wave, you would see companies develop stories about rooftop solar installations or green building attributes. These are not connected to a bigger goal or strategy and are communicated about in an ad hoc way, issued seemingly when the rest of the corporate communications team had a content hole to fill with some "feel good" content.

Strategic transparency is both annual and integrated across multiple channels including a robust section of the company website dedicated to ESG content that is tied to corporate strategy, long term commitments and interim progress against time bound targets. Both progress and challenges within the sustainability program are a regular part of quarterly investor meetings and can be found on packaging or in social media posts. This includes publishing a comprehensive annual ESG report that features not only the anecdotal stories of projects or programs completed during the reporting period, but also the year-over-year analysis of progress made, or not, against science-based targets that include timebound metrics.

The highest state of transparent leadership expands to ongoing communications with all stakeholders in a designed feedback loop that seeks to engage and include all the groups that a brand depends upon for meeting its purpose. In addition to integrated communications, there are carefully curated intake sessions with key stakeholders to foster two-way communication and produce feedback that helps with rapid retooling when roadblocks or barriers are encountered.

Position

The position a brand takes on any material or social issue is the final dimension on the continuum. Ranging from reactive to proactive, how a company chooses to show up when it comes to matters of injustice or exploitation can be the most obvious example of a say/do gap. The place where this dimension is easiest to understand is in social issues like racial justice, LGBTQ+ legislation, voter rights, or acknowledging heritage months like June Pride Month. Not only does the communication need to be authentic and transparent but the actual corporate policy, programs, resources, and reactions need to be consistent.

At the one end is reactive—these brands do not have any department resources dedicated to monitoring or understanding social issues. They adhere to regulatory requirements like reporting on the diversity of their workforce which is required by US, UK, and EU governing bodies. But it stops there. No acknowledgment of Black History Month or Pride. No HR policy for same sex marriage benefits. No allocation of parental leave for all parents, just mothers.

A follower brand will have policies and programs in place but will wait to see what other are doing before aligning behind a particular cause. Even the very early Renew100 coalition, where companies pledge to seek 100 per cent of their purchased energy from renewable sources, had a small number of signatories. Watching that organization grow over time, an observable pattern emerged that is true across other coalitions. A few brands across a handful of industries lead. Then another tranche of followers in those sectors will sign on. And then, sector by sector you will see others join to be the first in their industry.

Industry sector leaders tend to take a position or communicate a stance on a particular issue because it has direct correlation to circumstances that are both particular and familiar.

In the final category of leader, Ben & Jerry's is one of the best examples of a company who takes a position on social issues with a proactive and multidimensional approach. This is the core of their purpose. They are the only company I have every worked with who has a staff of activists and issue experts whose job is to help understand and advance a theory of change. Much like NGOs and activist groups, these subject matter experts at Ben & Jerry's give the ice cream maker a way to understand the issue they decide to engage with. This makes them not only a great ice cream maker but a social change leader as well:

> Guided by our Core Values, we seek in all we do, at every level of our business, to advance human rights and dignity, support social and economic justice for historically marginalized communities, and protect and restore the Earth's natural systems. In other words: we use ice cream to change the world.
>
> (Ben & Jerry's, 2022)

Another "Aha" Moment

I remember sitting in an expansive conference room at a global advertising company, situated near Madison Avenue in New York City. We overlooked Central Park and the view from my expensive and comfortable executive chair was breathtaking. Back in the late 2000s, I was there to discuss how the agency might want to consider adding a sustainability initiative to its service offerings. I had had my spear-in-the-chest moment, started my own boutique consulting firm, and was looking to partner with the likes of the large firm I had left in deploying a sustainability lens to communications and marketing.

That same year, 2007, the television show *Mad Men* debuted on AMC and became an instant hit. According to the pilot episode, the phrase "mad men" was a slang term coined in the 1950s by advertisers working on Madison Avenue to refer to themselves, "mad" being short for "Madison" (Witchel, 2008). And here I was, sitting in the *Mad Men* milieu, pitching what was really the antithesis of our communications industry. As illuminated in the 2007 documentary *Story of Stuff*, we had become a society with a linear and extractive economy. Creator Annie Leonard presents a critical vision of consumerist society, primarily American, under the conditions of globalization. Through simple cartoon graphics and her narration, she explains how we extract raw materials out of the ground, turn them into goods which, once used, are thrown away. Planned and perceived obsolescence.

As I met with resistance from the executives I was pitching, I had an "Aha" moment. The very industry I belonged to—marketing, advertising, persuasion—was responsible for fixing what we had wrought. It was no surprise that we were in the midst of both glorifying and examining the perils of the mad men era. I think we were, or at least I know I was, readying ourselves for a critical look at the reality that we had helped create. A throwaway society.

But my "Aha" was not just a dark realization of our culpability. Rather, it was a realization that persuasion is a powerful force for change. If we could turn a culture that, up until the 1950s, had rewarded thrift and prized the longevity of items into one that designed perceived obsolescence, then we could change it back. And that is at the heart of what purposeful brands are trying to do. Invent products and services that honor planetary resources and seek an equitable society with an awareness that even as we innovate, we have to bring our customers along with us. We will need to retrain everyone everywhere that there is no "away" where used things magically go when we're done with them. That low-cost items usually mean workers have been exploited somewhere in the process.

That we are more than our stuff.

From that moment on, it felt good to be a communicator, even if the executives didn't agree with me that day. They eventually came around.

References

Ben & Jerry's (2022) We believe that ice cream can change the world, Ben & Jerry's, www.benjerry.com/values (archived at https://perma.cc/KB46-YKQY)

Giridharadas, A (2022) Like capitalism itself, business journalism is broken. Can it be fixed? The Ink, https://the.ink/p/like-capitalism-itself-business-journalism (archived at https://perma.cc/5HNS-EB32)

Recycling Partnership, The (2019) America's leading beverage companies unite to reduce new plastic use and increase collection of their valuable bottles through "Every Bottle Back" initiative, The Recycling Partnership, https://recyclingpartnership.org/everybottleback (archived at https://perma.cc/PT8B-GDAA)

Skees, S (2019) The future? Yes—and. Business as a force for change, TED, www.ted.com/talks/sandy_skees_the_future_yes_and_business_as_a_force_for_change (archived at https://perma.cc/3WSC-MU3J)

Starbucks (2022) Coffee, Starbucks, www.starbucks.com/responsibility/sourcing/coffee (archived at https://perma.cc/CH5V-Q9R5)

Steffen, A (2022) Old thinking will break your brain: Why updating the way we look at the world is so critical now, and so hard, and how we can get better at doing it, Alex Steffen, https://alexsteffen.substack.com/p/old-thinking-will-break-your-brain (archived at https://perma.cc/628S-4M8T)

Witchel, A (2008) "Mad Men" has its moment, New York Times, www.nytimes.com/2008/06/22/magazine/22madmen-t.html (archived at https://perma.cc/33Y8-2DB9)

Closing the Say/ 04
Do Gap

Assessing Authenticity in Purpose

After the murder of George Floyd in Minneapolis in May of 2020, many companies began making pledges to support Black communities, to show up in solidarity against violence and racism. A flurry of social media posts, and first-ever corporate acknowledgment of Juneteenth began to get the attention of employees and customers.

As my colleague Conroy Boxhill likes to say, "Now, they're asking for the receipts." People began doing their research and calling out companies who were speaking up against racism but had not put their own houses in order. Social media lit up with posts about companies whose performative support of anti-racism was juxtaposed against the reality of an all-white board or an all-white C-suite. Digging deeper into ESG reports or other publicly available DEI documents, stakeholders were calling out those companies whose operations were not aligned with their public statements. This is a stark example of the say/do gap.

As we explored in earlier chapters, when defining purpose or a sustainability strategy, your first assessment must be internal. If we want to work toward a greater good as a brand, how are we doing with our own operations? Our employees? Our suppliers?

When the gap between what you are doing and what you are saying about it is large, you are greenwashing. When your walk gets ahead of your talk, you are green hushing. Both are dangerous for your brand but also, for the world at large.

Green Hushing

Green hushing does not get as much attention as greenwashing, but it has an equally chilling effect on progress. When companies are overly cautious about what they are willing to share regarding their sustainability journey and the barriers faced, mistakes made, challenges encountered, they participate in a failure to move everyone forward. Transparent communication about the hard parts of creating a greater good give everyone permission to try, to keep trying. That's why green hushing is harmful to the world.

But it's also harmful to the company who are not getting credit for the good work they are doing. Many stakeholders and most customers want to work for, buy from, invest in companies that have a purpose and are creating products that don't harm the environment. The only way for stakeholders to know what a brand is doing is for the brand to tell them, through a sustainability report, through stories on social media, via speeches and investor briefings. To not do so is green hushing.

A data center client asked us for an analysis of why their strong renewable energy program and significant ESG efforts were not receiving higher ratings from a variety of ranking agencies. Our report back, following an extensive internal assessment, competitive benchmarking, media scan, and interviews with rating agencies, revealed that the primary reason was lack of communication. Because many ranking agencies use data scrapers and web crawlers to pull information off publicly available information, the company was not being found effectively. Static information available only on the pages of a ESG report in PDF form, especially one that is several clicks away from the front page of a company website, are not found by data scrapers. To improve scores—beyond ensuring your work is good—companies need active, updated, searchable information that is conveyed across owned, earned, and paid channels.

There is another danger to green hushing—lack of transparency. I've been in many conference rooms or on zoom calls where I hear, "We're a humble company. We don't like to brag about our accomplishments, we prefer to let them speak for themselves."

First, I find this statement to be somewhat questionable since these same companies are very vocal when it comes to reporting on financial accomplishments, or touting revenue windfalls. They are, in fact, not quiet at all (their word is humble) when they hit a revenue milestone, win a large contract, or lure away a top executive from a competitor.

What they are, when it comes to communicating goals or progress on environmental or social programs is either unfamiliar or uncomfortable with new language. Or they are unwilling to face the scrutiny from stakeholders for a program that is not far along the leadership continuum.

Regardless of the reason, companies that maintain a certain level of muteness around sustainability programs will eventually be accused of deliberate obfuscation. Lack of transparency about goals, targets, progress, challenges, or pivots will eventually catch up to companies. As the ESG landscape continues to mature and disclosure requirements increase, there will be increasing regulatory requirements alongside stakeholder expectations for transparency.

Regulatory Disclosure

In 2022 the US Securities and Exchange Commission (SEC) continued to formalize and tighten its climate disclosure requirements with a new rule that requires public companies to provide detailed reporting of their climate-related risks, emissions, and net-zero transition plans. This rule change is in response to sustainability becoming a critical consideration for organizations today. Close to $5 trillion annually will be invested in sustainability by 2025—the largest capital reallocation in history. Additionally, investor scrutiny of climate risk is rising, in parallel with the rise in consumers and employees increasingly factoring sustainability into their decisions.

Experts compare this expansion of investor interest in sustainability and ESG to the early days of digital when the addition of technology was seen as a critical business element to every aspect of business. Over decades, technology became embedded into every function. In the same way, we sustainability experts expect environmental and social dimensions will also become an integrated component to every business function. This will be the direct outcome of realizing that the true cost of doing business must include effects on planetary resources and the strength of social constructs.

This doesn't mean, as some have predicted, that eventually when sustainability is embedded into business decisions, we will see chief sustainability officers and ESG departments go away. If we look at finance and digital as examples, once those dimensions are fully integrated into every aspect of business functionality, we see robust departments, specialization, regulations, and industry sectors grow up around them. This is what is happening now as we watch sustainability and ESG—as means of operationalizing purpose—widen, expand, become better funded and visible. We are watching the birth and growth of a new business disciple and profession.

As an example, the move toward greater company climate disclosure has gone global. The US SEC follows the United Kingdom, New Zealand, Japan, Hong Kong, and the EU's similar measures that require mutual climate risk disclosure. The Task Force on Climate-related Financial Disclosures (TCFD) issued voluntary guidelines that 2,600 companies around the world endorsed in 2021. Most institutional investors are citing climate risk as a leading issue driving their engagement with companies, and in 2021, the International Financial Reporting Standards Foundation (IFRS) created the International Sustainability Standards Board (ISSB) which will also release guidelines (Corb et al, 2022).

Many companies have been reporting their climate risk, mitigation, and footprint, across their entire value chain, for decades thanks to frameworks such as the Carbon Disclosure Project (CDP) and Dow Jones Sustainability Indices (DJSI). What the SEC and international regulations will require is not that different from these proposed standards. Earlier US laws such as Comprehensive Capital Analysis and Review (CCAR) and the Sarbanes-Oxley Act took many years to figure out, and climate disclosure will likely be a similar situation.

Greenwashing

After COP26, many companies experienced some backlash when it came to climate commitments and the scrutiny (earned or not) that brands face when they make net-zero promises is growing. Porter

Novelli research has found that 83 percent of Americans said they feel better about companies making bold environmental commitments, another 39 percent said they had researched a company's support of social and environmental issues. But it's not just the consumer taking a magnifying glass to green pledges. There are increasing pressures from investors to governmental regulations and independent ranking and rating organizations (Porter Novelli, 2021; Skees, 2022).

Companies are facing increased investigations into their strategies, plans, and commitments to reduce their GHG emissions—not just get to net-zero, which can be overly reliant on carbon offsets. Stakeholders are looking for details and plans that show how progress will be made now, not just backloading progress into the final years of a time bound commitment. The difference between companies that get called out and companies that do it right is how they communicate their plans.

There are a couple of companies laying it all out on the table with transparent reporting from the top down.

In its annual sustainability report, Ford publicized its target to become carbon neutral by 2050. Ford will focus on three sectors that account for around 95 percent of its CO_2 emissions to meet its goal: vehicle use, supply base, and company facilities. Not only is the automobile company investing $22 billion in electric vehicles through 2025, but Ford is also being explicit in the challenge of its supply chain. Ford said it would engage with suppliers to understand their collective environmental footprint, assist chosen suppliers in reducing emissions through its Partnership For a Cleaner Environment initiative and continue to interact with automotive industry partners to minimize supplier emissions.

PwC also reaffirmed its global objective in 2022 for reaching net-zero by 2030 and stressing the need to "build trust with stakeholders" and deliver sustained outcomes. Like Ford, in its effort to affect change outside of the organization, PwC will be supporting its clients to help reduce their emissions as well. Bob Moritz, Global Chairman of the PwC network, stated that "The business community has a responsibility to act, and we are determined to play our part, not just in our own operations and supply chain, but also in the way we advise and support our clients to create a sustainable world for future generations" (PwC, 2022).

It seems as if every company with a sustainability/ESG program has released a net-zero goal and this has now become table stakes for companies' climate strategies. These commitments have affected corporate communications and marketing departments by increasing pressure to expand messaging frameworks to include both specific data as well as anecdotal stories that bring climate progress to life. As well as help brands get credit for the good work they are doing.

If a company overstates or does not have clear, factual, and constant communications about climate commitments, it is greenwashing.

The biggest component of the say/do gap is the *doing* part of that equation. Something that requires a massive culture change inside a company. For brands to live up to their purpose, to deliver on their sustainability strategy and meet their ESG metrics, every decision needs to be made with the environment or society within the consideration set.

How does a company create a sustainability culture? Who is involved and what roles do they play?

> Leaders need to embrace an intentional enterprise redesign, what we call really "green sheeting" your company end to end, and the action needs to happen at pace. It will require considerable problem-solving to reach net-zero in the timeframe to which most people have committed. The time between now and 2030 is critical from a planet perspective and what you do over the next few years will be decisive.
>
> Lauren Corb, McKinsey (Corb et al, 2022)

Internal Change Management

The challenge is to integrate sustainability into an organization's DNA so that everyone thinks and acts with sustainability in mind. There are a few essential elements of a sustainability culture, beginning with and understanding that it is necessary to start in a small number of areas that are integrally linked to the business from which you can build a sense of sustainability ownership at every level of the organization.

Building a sustainability culture will be affected by where a brand is in its purpose journey once a sustainability strategy has been developed. This will dictate the extent of cultural change required to meet ambitions and targets. As we explored in Chapter 3, companies can be in a compliance, programmatic, strategic, or leadership stage overall—and these will also vary among issues. Some companies may want to simply increase the emphasis on sustainability in the culture, others may want a deeper shift involving realigning the company around a societal purpose, and others may be seeking a full transformation of their business (and therefore culture) as a matter of survival.

According to the 2022 Globescan–SustainAbility Institute annual research report *Sustainable Leaders*, over 700 global leaders from all over the world are seeing actions from institutional leaders, both corporations and NGOs, as more important than goals or ambitions (GlobeScan, 2022). Increasingly, companies are mostly considered leaders for putting sustainability at the core of their business models and strategies. Most striking is that 96 percent of the experts cited climate change as the most urgent issue facing companies, governments, and NGOs, with some social issues failing in urgency as environmental issues, including energy access, water and soil, are increasing.

Start With Purpose

Purpose is the North Star that guides all aspects of a company's strategy. When people understand the "why," they can take it with them in everything they do. Purpose is also not just something to help guide board and senior management decisions—it should be reflected in the "micro-decisions" made by employees at all levels if it is to ring true.

Understanding why a company exists is also a catalyst for innovation and creating business opportunities—and for getting employees excited about new growth opportunities for the business. Making it a part of what everyone does every day is where purpose comes to life. It's where purpose intersects not only with sustainability and ESG but also product development, marketing, sales, and customer relations.

Establish a Working Group

It is critical to have a team that is responsible for leading the effort to drive a sustainability culture, and either the CEO or Sustainability is best suited to lead the drive toward a sustainability culture. While CEO leadership on sustainability is critical, it must go beyond a single CEO. For the culture change to be genuine and durable, it must last more than one CEO's tenure. A CEO transition, even if planned, is one of the most significant events that a company can face, and potentially one of the most disruptive. When there is change at the top, it is important to make sure that sustainability is highlighted in the transition and to include signals that sustainability is not a remnant of an old regime but a vital part of a company that is forging ahead.

Build Out the Governance

Good governance is the key to any company achieving its purpose and successfully integrating sustainability strategy and ESG programs in service to that purpose. It is also critical to hold departments like R&D, innovation, procurement, supply chain, or manufacturing accountable to helping meet key goals and KPIs. Governance is simply the structure put in place to ensure the right policies, resources, expectations, and accountability systems are functioning. This can include the formation of a cross-company steering committee, integration into the annual budgeting cycles, decision-making processes, and clear accountability for meeting departmentally allocated portions of topline climate or DEI goals.

Focus, Focus, Focus

Focus on a few, key topics where you can have the greatest impact—competitive differentiators that sets your organization apart in the marketplace. A great example of cohesive and comprehensive change that is focused in three key areas is General Mills. Through its

Accelerate strategy to drive shareholder value, it is committed to and regularly reports on the progress it makes in building its brands, innovating, unleashing its scale and being a force for good. Its portfolio of brands includes household names such as Cheerios, Nature Valley, Blue Buffalo, Häagen-Dazs, Old El Paso, Pillsbury, Betty Crocker, Yoplait, Annie's, Wanchai Ferry, Yoki, and more.

Within its Accelerate strategy is the Force for Good pillar that houses all their environmental and social commitments and strategies. According to comments made in a February investor meeting, Jeff Harmening, CEO, describes how they will ensure full integration across the business: "To improve the integration of ESG into our business, we formed a new Global Impact Governance Committee, which is accountable for ensuring our global responsibility programs are resourced, on track, and, ultimately, achieved" (General Mills, 2022).

The most important aspect of the General Mills approaches to operationalizing purpose through Force for Good is the top-down, bottom-up approach they take with a clear focus on their top three commitments: GHG emission reduction, expansion of regenerative agriculture, and recycled packaging. They have deployed a company-wide initiative to inspire employees and help them understand why Global Impact initiatives matter, educate them on General Mills' commitments, and explain how new operating models require all employees to act differently across the enterprise.

Start Internal, Show External Pressure

When rolling out a sustainability culture initiative, incorporate external as well as internal views. Ensuring that people understand the importance of sustainability to key external stakeholders such as investors, customers, and business partners makes clear that this is not a vanity "do good" project for senior management.

In addition to involving external stakeholders, be sure to involve employees in the process of creating your sustainability culture. This ongoing co-creation is critical to ensuring the cultural changes are authentic and durable.

A climate workshop with multiple functions represented yielded unique insights from legal and HR. This approach helped to reinforce the power of teams, collaboration, and the notion that everyone has a role to play in being an "ESG ambassador" and in bringing the company's sustainability strategy to life.

Sustainability as the Great Connector

In almost every case, CSOs and sustainability managers are more widely integrated across the company than almost any other function. When I work with internal leaders, it's not unusual for them to be in regular communications and depend upon monthly engagement with departments across the organization. From procurement to product design, from finance to HR, from philanthropy to the board of directors, sustainability team members are in regular contact. At a minimum, they are interviewing their colleagues for input and data that will be included in the annual ESG report. Beyond that, they are looking for pockets of influence to help direct goals, drive behavior change, seed initiatives for progress against GHG emissions targets, or improve DEI metrics.

In cases where these individuals are most successful, they have a combination of persuasive talent, clear lines of authority, credibility, business knowledge, fluency in sustainability, and communication skills. They are adroit at building a network of relationships across the company to influence, inspire, and educate at multiple levels.

Comprehensive Change Management

When implementing change management as a means of closing the say/do gap, there are three integrated objectives that underpin any strategy. The first is "engage". Be sure that people understand the learning objective and are inspired to take part. The second, "participate", ensures that people take part, apply knowledge, practice, and learn from each other. The third is "activate". People need to feel confident and supported so that they can apply what they've learned.

The unique challenge in driving purpose commitments across a company is lack of awareness and shared vocabulary. When we think about other enterprise change programs, like building a safety culture or driving quality through initiatives like Six Sigma, the fundamentals are shared. We all know what safety means, even if there are intricacies associated with how we keep employees safe or the behaviors we need to see in order to achieve a reduction in injuries. Similarly with quality; everyone understands the concept of quality even if how processes get defined by Six Sigma—a point where only 3.4 errors per one million process events result in a defect—is not widely known. So, the roll out of a quality improvement or safety program begins with a universal understanding of the concepts and end results sought.

Not so with purpose and sustainability. First, there is much confusion, as we've noted, on how purpose is applied to a business alongside mission and vision. Second, there are overlapping definitions for sustainability and ESG that get intermingled with concepts like GHG, carbon emissions, and climate change. In every case, we are not starting with some sort of universal and shared definition.

A secondary but no less important consideration is how wide purpose and sustainability must get driven across the company. Safety and quality are primarily manufacturing processes with ancillary implications across a company. ESG issues are widespread and, as we have shown, purpose is a central belief and commitment to a greater good that has implications on each and every dimension of a business.

One of the components is showcasing an ongoing and strong declaration from the CEO and senior leaders, and clearly shows the connection between purpose and business strategy. Repeatedly, we see the need for a top-down and bottom-up approach. Leadership must become a vocal and constant advocate and champion of purpose and sustainability deployment. An executive interviewed as part of the change process was asked to describe how the company would look different after a year of this change program. The answer was so simple and yet hard to envision. "When we begin every leadership update meeting with how we are meeting our environmental or social commitments, rather than financials, then I'll know we've seen real change."

Can you imagine quarterly strategy updates or monthly business update meetings that begin with GHG emissions updates or pay gap equity results, rather than the litany of revenue, margin, cost we are accustomed to? As we explored that executive's answer, we began to understand just how pervasive a change needs to happen. Somehow, closing the say/do gap means increasing our language about business metrics to include progress against clearly understood targets and their quarterly increments in achieving things like net-zero emissions or zero waste to landfill.

Having a CEO and leaders who address these KPIs with the same scrutiny and vigor as earnings before interest, taxes, and amortization (EBITA) is what real change looks like. This type of top-down signal of importance and fluency in non-financial performance indicators is an integral part of a change management program.

Clear, simple, human language that explains the purpose, sustainability, and ESG in a way everyone can understand is another critical component. This is the art and science of sustainability communication. There are technical terms and specifics that must be included to avoid the serious issue of greenwashing—which is regulated by the Federal Trade Commission's *Green Guide* (2022).

According to the Federal Trade Commission, the *Green Guides* were first issued in 1992 and provide guidance on general principles that apply to all environmental marketing claims. They provide guidance on how consumers are likely to interpret claims and how marketers can substantiate these claims. Lastly, they show marketers the best ways to qualify their claims to avoid deceiving consumers. There is also guidance on marketers' use of product certifications and seals of approval, claims about materials and energy sources that are "renewable," and "carbon offset" claims.

Just like the need for CEO and leadership fluency and consistency in addressing purpose progress, the internal communications department needs to maintain a regular drumbeat, so purpose doesn't become a "flavor of the month" topic. It is important to make it part of everyday conversation among all employees. In the same way Slack channels and Yammer groups trade stories about big deals secured, management changes, new products being launched, you want stories to be shared about climate progress or packaging innovation as well.

Internal communications calendars and social posts can find the bright spots—showcasing successes to employees builds momentum and demonstrates how the company is closing its own say/do gap. However, it is important to prioritize and sequence these activities so they match the cadence of change management rollout. Every commitment will have its own unique process on the companywide purpose journey. Some changes will be easier to create, be less resistant to change, be more tightly aligned to business strategy. Others will be more hidden or more abstract and the communication will need to reflect that nuance.

Lastly, use a tiered approach to segment the learning strategy and deploy by population and commitment. Even when change is desired across the entire organization, there will be pockets of people in adjacent departments who will be more directly impacted and whose buy-in will be more material than others. Start with those change agents or influencers who are a critical path to acceptance. Start there.

The Power of Branding and Language

Companies are used to providing ongoing communications across their channels regarding business updates, product marketing, brand advertising. But what's been missing is a comprehensive communications plan that expands this language of business to include goals, progress, challenges, and anecdotes about how a company is operating across its entire ESG continuum.

Also, it is important to remember that across every stakeholder group there will be a spectrum of knowledge, interest, and technical expertise when it comes to the very detailed aspects of greenhouse gas emissions, waste, chemicals, water, as well as the physics and scientific aspects of sustainability. This makes communications especially tricky. It means taking highly dense technical sustainability information and turning it into something that is easily digestible for many audiences.

While there is no perfect formula, here are some things to consider when building out your next ESG communications initiative.

First, it's nothing new. Sustainability communications components are the same as any comprehensive program. A best practice is to develop a platform that provides a cohesive wrapper and rationale to which the entire spectrum of sustainability commitments and ESG programs can be authentically linked and understood. Sustainability and ESG communications success can also be measured just as all communications are measured (e.g., Who did we reach? How do they feel about us as a company and about our products?).

Data and storytelling are essential. Rating and ranking indices are constantly scrapping data for algorithm assessments of a company's performance against climate commitments, emissions, waste, water, diversity in leadership, supply chain risk, and more. A sustainability comms program needs to be comprehensive, transparent, rooted in data provided on a regular and findable basis, and include the aspirational and anecdotal stories that bring it to life. From there, the ESG content becomes a real-time look at specific updates on progress.

Think big. It's important to provide a big picture vision of what you want to achieve, supported by measurable goals and objectives. Like setting performance targets against a long-term vision, the new opportunity is connecting the dots and integrating sustainability with this high-level business strategy. And tell the story repeatedly, with a constant cadence, to the broadest range of stakeholders.

A global information center is an internal knowledge resource that can be an essential component of helping drive change across an organization. Think of this like an "innovation center." It can be both a physical location with tangible examples of packaging innovation or energy efficiency tips, or a living demonstration facility where employees and the media can come to see real world examples of sustainability programs in action. It can also be an online resource where any employee can search by topic for deeper information about goals, targets or the specifics of a particular company commitment or program. It is also a great place to provide books, podcasts, continuing education programs, and other deep technical sources that interested employees can explore to their hearts' content.

Once people begin to understand climate change and the challenges facing every company, many want to go deeper and learn more. A global resource center is a great way to help educate and bring more further along the knowledge spectrum—enhancing progress on company goals.

References

Corb, L, Henderson, K, Koller, T, and Venugopal, S (2022) Understanding the SEC's proposed climate risk disclosure rule, McKinsey, www. mckinsey.com/capabilities/strategy-and-corporate-finance/our-insights/ understanding-the-secs-proposed-climate-risk-disclosure-rule (archived at https://perma.cc/XDW6-BVPX)

Federal Trade Commission (2022) Environmentally friendly products: FTC's Green Guides, FTC, www.ftc.gov/news-events/topics/truth-advertising/green-guides (archived at https://perma.cc/7NV3-AQ9Q)

General Mills (2022) Force for good, General Mills, https://s29.q4cdn. com/993087495/files/doc_events/2022/05/04/General-Mills-Force-For-Good-2022-Transcript.pdf (archived at https://perma.cc/MB85-XQ5D)

Globescan (2022) *Sustainability Leaders*, GlobeScan-SustainAbility Survey, www.sustainability.com/globalassets/sustainability.com/thinking/ pdfs/2022/gss-sustainability-leaders-2022.pdf (archived at https://perma. cc/858F-9J6Y)

Porter Novelli (2021) Introducing the Porter Novelli focus: Business action for climate crisis, PN, www.porternovelli.com/findings/introducing-the-porter-novelli-focus-business-action-for-climate-crisis (archived at https:// perma.cc/T9AK-T6CP)

PwC (2022) Environment, PwC, www.pwc.com/gx/en/about/corporate-sustainability/environmental-stewardship.html (archived at https:// perma.cc/B3NF-B2S6)

Skees, S (2022) Companies who communicate breakthrough when facing greenwashing scrutiny, www.porternovelli.com/intelligence/2022/02/11/ companies-who-communicate-breakthrough-when-facing-greenwashing-scrutiny (archived at https://perma.cc/PB6S-85Z7)

Unlocking Innovation and Creativity

05

"Yes—and" Thinking Can Solve Sustainability Challenges

CVS Health's move to eliminate all tobacco products from every store in 2014 was years in the making and was designed to crystallize the company's ambition to move from predominantly a retail pharmacy to a national healthcare company. According to Eileen Howard Boone, who was Senior Vice President of Corporate Social Responsibility and Philanthropy for CVS Health during the years before and after the tobacco removal:

> The decision came out of a realization that not only was the sale of tobacco products a barrier to the future growth of the company as a trusted healthcare provider, but also cigarettes—which remain the leading preventable cause of death—had no place in a setting where healthcare was delivered.
>
> (Boone, 2018)

CVS's decision to remove all tobacco products from its store meant the company had to walk away from what, at the time, was $2 billion in annual sales. Not an insignificant amount. However, the team at CVS were willing to look squarely at what it meant to the business if they were going to live out a purpose committed to healthcare. The company also made the decision to publicly announce their decision—taking full advance of the moment to reinforce their purpose and commitments. Three years later, CVS reported that overall sales were up in its stores thanks to new business that came its way from the US Affordable Care Act and the company's new profile as a pharmacy benefit management entity, as well as its growing medical services business (Japsen, 2014).

CVS saw a significant uptick in health partnerships with groups like the Department of Veterans Affairs and UCLA Health, according to Boone (2018): "The fact that companies and consumers now see us as a convenient and affordable point of access for quality care creates longer-term growth opportunities for our business."

This is just one of innumerable examples of brands that flips significant environmental or social challenges into opportunities for innovation. We looked in a previous chapter at Starbucks' example of building a more reliable and resilient coffee supply chain through the invention of a fairtrade system. I've often heard sustainability thought leaders proclaim that the best place to look for innovation opportunities is where you have your greatest challenge or where there is significant friction in the supply chain. Additionally, places for innovation can be where costs and carbon emissions are high. For example, switching to biochemicals—using what is increasingly known as "green chemistry"—will mean a reduction in greenhouse gas emissions for both the manufacturing process and within the product specifications. It can also mean a reduction in cost since there are many complexities associated with the handling of toxic chemicals in production that have labor and disposal ramifications.

A materiality assessment can sometimes uncover places for innovation, but in my experience these analyses are better at revealing risk and enterprise-level challenges. Sometimes, the place for innovation is elsewhere, such as in product design, new market opportunities, expanded customer engagement, compelling advertising content, or supply chain expansion.

Starting with Compliance as a Driver

When companies begin looking for innovation opportunities, a good first place comes from the constraints created by the regulatory landscape. Whether it is worker safety or careful disposal of hazardous waste, being compliant to a range of legal requirements can produce a pain point that sustainability innovation can address.

It is important to recognize that environmental regulations vary by country, by state or region, and even by city. Some companies look at the most stringent regulations and where those are likely headed as an initial framing. The consideration is how to get ahead of regulatory requirements by exceeding even the most restrictive, in order to reduce complexity in operational response. For example, in 2007 San Francisco banned single use plastic bags in groceries. By April of 2008, Whole Foods announced a national ban on plastic bags, and by 2014 one-third of Californians lived in cities with plastic bag bans (Larson and Venkova, 2014). Whether outright bans or legislation requiring the collection of bag fees, a scattering of municipal regulations began a cascading series of considerations by grocery chains to add paper bags or reusable alternatives that is still in play in 2022. Wegmans announced it would complete the elimination of plastic bags in its stores at the end of 2022 in Virginia and North Carolina locations (Rubak, 2022).

Brands can also be pressured by voluntary codes that stakeholders expect them to comply with—overall operation frameworks like the Greenhouse Gas Protocol, or industry-specific ones, such as the Forest Stewardship Council (FSC) require more than legal compliance in most countries. Both frameworks, one for calculating carbon emissions and the other used by timber companies to report on how they manage their tree crops, are voluntary. There are no laws requiring companies to report on or adhere to the guidelines and requirements contained in these protocols. What they do, however, is give companies universally accepted management systems that provide consistent rigor and transparency across multiple borders when it comes to these two environmental practices. In many cases, the requirement to become FSC certified will be a more comprehensive set of requirements that may otherwise be stipulated by local logging laws.

Extended Producer Responsibility

Extended producer responsibility (EPR) is a good example of regulatory constraints that have driven sustainability innovation. It is responsible for manufacturers' efforts to tackle packaging or explore product take-back initiatives as a way of meeting a growing range of regulations that place responsibility for product end of life on the original manufacturer. EPR is a discipline that adds all of the environmental costs associated with a product throughout the product life cycle—specifically its end of life—to the market price of that product. Many countries and local municipalities have passed legislation that places responsibility for the recovery and handling of no longer used products in the hands of the brand who originally made the product. The concept holds that manufacturers should bear a significant degree of responsibility for the environmental impacts of their products throughout the product life cycle, including upstream impacts from the selection of materials for the products, impacts from manufacturers' production process itself, and downstream impacts from the use and disposal of the products.

Since 1994, the Organisation for Economic Co-operation and Development (OECD), an international organization of countries and citizens developing policies and standards that address social, economic, and environmental challenges, has driven EPR policy change in almost all its 38 member countries (OECD, 2022). The focus of its work has been to develop regulatory frameworks that move financial responsibility to private sector enterprises for managing their products at the post-consumer phase. Doing so, it serves as a guard rail that can significantly reduce the municipal waste stream. When Thomas Lindquist first introduced the concept of EPR in Sweden in 1990, he proposed that product manufacturers and distributors should be responsible for the life of their products and packaging after the consumer is through with them (OECD, 2001).

This is where innovation comes in. When using an EPR filter, producers accept their responsibility for designing products that minimize life cycle environmental impacts, which can include how a product meets the regulatory requirements for end of life. But regulation is just one forcing mechanism. From a brand perspective, here is where a close connection to both purpose and sustainability strategy will be useful in determining how much ambition to place in product design for the end of life of a particular product.

Whether pressure for innovation is coming from mandatory, nego-tiated, or voluntarily accepted producer responsibility, it is important to take a look at the ways in which public policy and legislative rela-tions can intersect with sustainability innovation. Manufacturers are constantly faced with a far-reaching and fast-changing regulatory landscape. From a fiduciary perspective, corporations work to influ-ence the development of legislation that is going to have a material implication on sourcing, manufacturing processes or create a finan-cial liability if discarded products now become the burden of the company.

I worked with a household battery coalition on a consumer recy-cling campaign that was developed in parallel with a national and locally focused legislative effort. This industry group understood that for a national campaign encouraging people to recycle their used household batteries to be successful, we needed local municipalities to have the systems in place for collection and recycling. The goal was to get people to not just mix these batteries into their trash—or simply hoard them in boxes and bins in their garages—but separate them and bring them in for proper handling. A key part of the strat-egy was to monitor and help develop local municipal legislation that was harmonized across the United States and consistent with regula-tory frameworks in the European Union.

These global battery manufacturers were faced with a patchwork of different waste collection systems, a range of regulatory require-ments, and a hodgepodge of thresholds that had real, on-the-ground implications at landfills across the US. The goal of the campaign working group was twofold. They wanted to provide guidance and participate in the creation of a de facto national household battery recycling regulatory framework so that the manufacturers could ad-here to requirements in a holistic way nationally rather than individual programs deployed differently in every city or town. Additionally, they wanted to create a consumer campaign that helped people know what role they played in the successful collec-tion and disposal of spent single use batteries. This two-pronged approach was interdependent.

The tension between localized legislative requirements and the need for an efficient global take-back program requires collaboration between a company's public policy and legislative affairs teams as well as those doing product design, packaging, and on-pack copy development, and marketing and communications teams.

Sustainability innovation at the product level is challenging because of the complex interplay between internal and external pressures. There are several ways that a brand can explore EPR requirements as a place for innovation and consumer engagement. Let's take a look at a range of the types of EPR programmatic approaches that brands can explore when looking for ways to drive innovation that can solve environmental challenges:

- **Optional programs:** Producers offer to reuse and recycle components if customers so request. This is usually the first place that a brand begins experimenting with end of life concepts as a way of gauging consumer interest. A great example of this is the early 2022 announcement by Colgate that many of its toothpaste tubes are now fully recyclable (Colgate, 2022). According to the launch press release, "The pilot will focus on one county or municipality to test how educational efforts can build tube recycling rates and assess the quality of the tube material that is collected for reprocessing. The data will be used to define easy-to-action best practices for tube recycling to be shared with communities and recyclers around the country." Colgate is also sharing its recyclable tube expertise with other companies including competitors, through trade forums and individual meetings to accelerate a transition to recyclable tubes. The idea is to encourage the recycling community to add tubes to their lists of acceptable materials and create behavior change among consumers to recycle tubes.

- **Partnership programs:** These are government partnerships with producers for returning certain types of municipal waste to producers for remanufacturing, reuse, or recycling. Throughout many counties in the United States, there are programs like this for carpet and paint. In 2002, carpet manufacturers, several state environmental departments, fiber manufacturers and others in the carpet industry agreed to found and fund a non-profit entity to increase the landfill diversion, reuse, and recycling of waste carpet. Carpet American Recovery Effort has slowly increased the recovery and recycling of waste carpet (CARE, 2019). From 2002 to 2019, CARE partners had diverted over 5.6 billion gross pounds of post-consumer carpet from landfills in the United States. The paint industry has a similar public–private partnership, PaintCare (2022). A program from the American Coatings Association works with other product stewardship organizations like the Product Stewardship Institute and has advocated for paint recycling legislation across the US. By helping shape the laws, it ensures its member companies can formulate operational strategies that will help them comply with recycling regulations.

- **Mandatory take-back:** Once EPR laws have been passed by municipalities or at the state level, a system that supports producers who are required to take back products emerges as a solution for this new regulatory reality. This may apply to products that are particularly complex, dangerous to reuse, or bulky and cumbersome for consumers to manage at end of life. California's recently expanded Used Mattress Recovery and Recycling Act (SB 254) stipulates that all manufacturers are required by law to take back a customer's used mattress and/or box spring—at no cost to the consumer—when a new mattress and/or box spring is delivered. While these regulations are designed to deal with end of life, it is also important that these programs have a structure for regulatory oversight regarding the environmental and social components. In the California mattress law, the original stewardship plan relied too heavily on incineration—a diversion from landfill strategy that has negative GHG emissions implications. In 2017, the state revised the law to now discourage incineration and to set minimum goals for materials recovery that increase gradually over time (Mattress Recycling Council, 2022). The bedding industry's Mattress Recycling Council is a non-profit that operates state-wide mattress recycling programs in states that have passed EPR laws. Like the battery recycling group I worked with, this organization educates consumers in a wide range of states. It also provides, for a fee, a way for manufacturers to comply with the regulatory requirement for product take-back without needing to create their own reclamation system—trucks, collection centers, disassembly, and distribution of reclaimed materials for upcycling, including the incineration of any unusable remnants. Not to mention the requirement for tracking and maintaining a transparent chain of custody and reporting of the environmental impacts during each part of the recycling process.

- **Zero waste:** Theoretically, a circular economy is possible. One where every product can be disassembled or reconstituted in some way to become the material inputs for another manufacturing process. Or organic material can be returned as compost back into the natural world. The process of creating a circular product is complex. This may require brands to design products that can be fully recycled.

Designing for disassembly is a core principle of zero waste, since the easy collection, capture and rerouting of the various component parts of any product make getting those elements back into the resource stream easy. According to the World Business Council for Sustainable Development (WBCSD)'s circular economy practitioner guide, designing for disassembly involves some straightforward tactics, for example:

- The fewer parts you use, the fewer parts there are to take apart.
- As with parts, the fewer fasteners (e.g., glue, screws, etc.) used, the better.
- Common and similar fasteners that require only a few standard tools will help to simplify and speed disassembly.
- Screws are faster to unfasten than nuts and bolts.
- Glues should be avoided.
- Building disassembly instructions into the product will help users understand how to take it apart.

(WBCSD, 2018)

- **Value add:** The value-add dimension of extended producer responsibility in many cases looks more like a new business model than simply a redesigned product. What changes is how the manufacturer sees its extended responsibility for end of life as an opportunity for introducing products that are purchased in conjunction with a managed service with a monthly recurring fee. A great example is addressing the serious issue of electronics waste. Equipment failure along with the new-release-every-year product cycles creates massive amounts of electronics going to landfill each year. According to the United Nations, more than 53 million metric tonnes of e-waste was sent to landfills in 2019 (Forti et al, 2020).

Gerrard Street, headquartered in Amsterdam, The Netherlands, has developed a new business model for headphones that is working on the problem of e-waste. Their modular headphones are designed specifically for a subscription business model. The products were designed for easy disassembly and repair, and no glue is used making them. If a part fails, customers can simply order a new part, thus extending the lifetime of the headphones. The subscription model allows Gerrard Street to collect and reuse components from headphones once a customer has finished with them. Customers pay a monthly fee and can send headphones back to be repaired or upgraded as needed.

Each of these categories and examples take a "Yes—and" mindset. Product designers looking at disassembly, financial analysts exploring new business models, sourcing, and production line leads experimenting with new processes all have an open, nonbinary way of approaching the problem. How do we reduce or mitigate the environmental impact of making something even as we use materials and create products that have a life after their use? How do we do both?

Extended producer responsibility, circular economy, zero waste are all sustainability concepts that allow for innovation opportunities related to the environmental dimensions of a brand's footprint. There are ways for innovation to be applied to the social commitments and cultural engagements that a brand's purpose or sustainability strategy is attempting to improve.

"Yes—and" thinking can be applied to social challenges, cultural change, and shifting consumer expectations emerging as part of the cultural zeitgeist. When it comes to products, sometimes the best place for innovation is looking at the socio-cultural dimension of the product and exploring ways in which the brand can live up to its purpose or meet sustainability commitments for diversity, equity, inclusion, and justice. This includes looking at who the product is designed for, who makes the product, or how the product is marketed to a wider range of potential customers.

Exploring an All-Gender Landscape for Inclusive Innovation

The concept of nonbinary thinking, of a "Yes—and" mindset is rich with possibility. One issue that brings "Yes—and" thinking into the spotlight is gender.

Today's young people are beginning to reflect the full spectrum of identity, avoiding the binary constraints of generations past. Twenty-three percent of Gen Z expect to change their gender identity at least once in their lifetime, and only 44 percent say they only buy clothes designed for their gender (Irregular Labs, 2019). They're seeking out safe spaces to express themselves, especially online, and they want the things they consume—from media to beauty and fashion—to reflect their more fluid and diverse identities (Carmichael, 2022). Not only that, they're looking to employers to be inclusive in their hiring practices—88 percent of Gen Z believe it's important that potential employers ask their pronouns (including 65 percent who strongly agree it's important) and 25 percent say they would decline a job offer if they failed to use an applicant's pronouns (Tallo, 2020).

How we talk and think about gender matters, not just for a growing segment of our audiences, but for our businesses. Language is one of the most powerful tools we wield as humans. Language can create possibility, but it can also create constraints on how we think and importantly, how we identify ourselves and those around us.

Lisa Kenney is the CEO of Reimagine Gender and the former Executive Director of Gender Spectrum. Leveraging decades of corporate leadership experience, she has developed a body of work and discipline on the intersection of gender, identity, and orientation as well as how gender roles play out in corporate and market settings. Lisa and I have worked together on a number of projects that have helped companies understand gender and implement change across the organization.

It is important to pause and define terms. I have already alluded to the power of language, so clarity is essential for a topic so complex. Based on Lisa's work, we start with a level set about gender and identity. Discussions about gender are everywhere—from news feeds to movies and marketing. Before looking at what gender is, it is important to start with what gender is not, since that is often a source of confusion.

Sex

People tend to use the terms "sex" and "gender" interchangeably. But although connected, the two terms are not equivalent. Generally, a new-born child's sex is determined as either male or female (some US states and other countries offer a third option) based on a quick look at the baby's genitals at birth. This is often referred to as "sex assigned at birth." It is assumed, on the basis of someone's sex, that they will develop certain biological traits (levels of certain hormones, specific physical characteristics appearing around puberty, etc.). While we are often taught that bodies can be biologically either "female" or "male," there are Intersex traits (often identified later in life) that demonstrate that sex exists across a continuum of possibilities.

Often, people assume that someone's gender will align with their sex. For example, someone assigned as female at birth will be a woman. Sometimes this is true—in which case we refer to that person as "cisgender." But this is certainly not always the case. The female mentioned may have a nonbinary gender identity (e.g., genderqueer or genderfluid) rather than a binary gender identity (woman). You can never know someone's gender from their sex or vice versa.

Sexuality

Gender and sexuality are two distinct, but related, aspects of self. Gender is personal (how we see ourselves), while sexuality is interpersonal (whom we are physically, emotionally, and/or romantically attracted to). While these are two different aspects of who we are, our sexual orientation is related to gender because it is defined by our gender and the gender(s) of people we are attracted to. Because of this relationship, new gender identity terms have expanded the language of sexual identities as well.

Gay, straight, lesbian, and even bisexual are all terms based on binary gender identities. Nonbinary identities for gender require nonbinary terms for sexuality. For example, a woman who is interested in or open to men and nonbinary identified people might look for a way to communicate that in their identity. Pansexual is one identity that would fit that desire.

Three Dimensions of Gender

Whereas a person's sex relates to biology and physiology, gender refers to the roles, behaviors, identities, and types of expression a society creates for its people. A person's gender is the complex interrelationship between three dimensions: body, identity, and social (Reimagine Gender, 2022).

For example, females are biologically similar around the world. What it means to be a woman, however, evolves over time and is culturally specific. The expectations of what is appropriate for a woman differs throughout the world, and we can all think of ways that things are acceptable today that were not acceptable for a gender earlier in our lifetime.

Identities are the language we use to understand and communicate our gender. They typically fall into binary (e.g., man, woman, trans), nonbinary (e.g., genderqueer, genderfluid) and ungendered (e.g., agender, genderless) categories. The meaning associated with a particular identity can vary among individuals using the same term.

Gender is an inherent aspect of a person. Individuals do not choose their gender, nor can they be made to change it. The term someone uses to communicate their gender identity, however, may change over time as they mature and gain access to new language. As mentioned previously, a person's gender identity may correspond to or differ from their sex.

Social gender includes gender expression, roles, and expectations and how society uses them to try to enforce conformity to prevailing gender norms. Practically everything is given a gender—activities, careers, and clothes are some of the more obvious examples.

Expectations regarding gender are communicated through every aspect of our lives, including family, culture, peers, schools, community, media and religion. Although a society generally has prevailing gender norms, everyone's experiences of social gender will vary based on other aspects of self, since gender intersects with other aspects of who we are in terms of race, ethnicity, class, location, and religion, among others.

Gender, especially as it's been used historically, is often one of those constraints. When we think of and use gender as a binary—men/women, masculine/feminine—we reduce something incredibly complex into something easily digestible, but incomplete and limiting. And, while language is an attempt to organize and manage a world that can feel chaotic and confusing, our resistance to the fluid and ambiguous alienates us from what's most important about the full spectrum of human experience. There is so much more in the messy middle of life than on the poles.

Fifty-five percent of young people believe gender stereotypes exist partially because of the way companies have represented gender identity in marketing and advertising (Porter Novelli, 2021). Businesses must start to interrogate the ways in which they participate in and perpetuate gender cliches and biases through the products, campaigns, cultures, and decisions they make. A failure to do so will not only alienate them from a growing segment of the market, but also cut them off from opportunities for real brand growth and development.

From government policies requiring retailers to provide gender neutral toy sections, to the way in which gender and sex is reported in corporate data, gender is influencing business in new and increasingly relevant ways. But there is a way to navigate these changes. When you free yourself from the confines of binary gender thinking, you start to ask new questions and address challenges with greater freedom and flexibility. How does ideation look, feel, and sound when you no longer use outdated definitions of gender as a starting point when thinking about product design and user experience?

CASE STUDY   Meet Fluide: Beauty For All

Fluide is a mission-driven cosmetics brand that creates vegan, cruelty-free and paraben-free beauty products for all skin shades and gender expressions. Founders Isabella Giancarlo and Laura Kraber saw the ways the beauty industry propped up narrow definitions of gender. They knew the world needed more brands that addressed and celebrated the shifting landscape of identity and expression, especially among Gen Z (Leiva, 2018).

Building a brand outside the confines of gender allowed Giancarlo and Kraber to use inclusivity as a starting point, not an adaptation or evolution of their products. They also relied on their target audience to realize their vision, ensuring a true product–market fit from the beginning.

CASE STUDY   Hasbro: Come As You Are

In a recent Porter Novelli study, 60 percent of Gen Z respondents said they wished companies offered more products and services that were not marketed to only one gender, and 50 percent said they actually struggled to make a purchase because of products marketing to only one gender (2021). Iconic toy maker Hasbro addressed this tension head on—and it's worth quoting CEO, Brian Goldner, at length from an interview with The Hollywood Reporter:

> We look at our brands more inclusively than ever. In fact, we eliminated the old delineation of gender. And if you think about a brand, be it My Little Pony, where 30 percent of our global TV audience is boys, or Star Wars, where we are launching [all-female animated series] Forces of Destiny with Lucas and Disney, you're seeing people who want to be engaged in these stories.

(Siegel, 2017)

Hasbro reimagined the online shopping experience, changing how information is organized or searched. Out with the old (filtering by gender and age) and in with the new (brand based and a child's interests). By removing gendering obstacles for both children and parents when purchasing products they are most interested in, they free customers to experience a legacy brand in new ways. This un-gendering of the website has generated other changes in how Hasbro markets its toys. In 2021, the toy company announced it would be changing the names of iconic Mr and Mrs Potato Head to simply "Potato Head," and include a range of body parts, hair styles and accessories, giving children the opportunity to create potato versions of their own family, regardless of what they look like (Aquilina, 2021).

CASE STUDY   White Claw: Defying (and Redefining) a Category

White Claw spiked the nascent hard seltzer beverage category with its focus on a Millennial audience and a unique marketing campaign that did not specifically target men or women. Until 2018, hard seltzer in the US was a small category with names like Mike's Hard Lemonade, Smirnoff Ice, and Budweiser's Lime-a-rita. White Claw's entry drove the entire hard seltzer category—all while avoiding the gender stereotypes traditional in the beverage industry. Hard seltzer is usually marketed toward women (read: pink and peach, floral designs, slender typography). White Claw upended this positioning with their simple grey and white cans with non-gendered artwork of waves. Their wide appeal is perhaps best captured by their unofficial tagline: "Ain't no laws when you're drinking Claws!" (Heil, 2019).

It's not accurate to call this approach gender neutral—it simply doesn't include gender. Instead of alienating people with whom hyper-feminine branding doesn't resonate, they drove usage and brand loyalty across a wider, more diverse cohort. And, while we are far away from a post-gendered world, White Claw's focus on characteristics, rather than the tired gender stereotypes, is refreshingly good business. In my work with companies that want to explore how to apply an all gender (or none at all) to product design and market expansion, I have heard many anecdotes of lost sales due to a gendered purchase framework. Stories of men looking for pink sneakers but only finding them in the women's section because a product designer decided pink could not be a men's shoe. Or eyewear for broad face structures that can only be found in the men's section, regardless of the gender identity of the customer. In each case, the anecdotes created internal questions by product and marketing departments to take a fresh look at who they were designing for.

Brands that can expand their idea of gender and throw off its outdated constraints will not only align to an evolving customer and employee base, but also create business opportunities that are so well-illustrated by the brands highlighted previously. For companies, understanding and addressing gender isn't just about being inclusive. It's smart business.

Looking at gender is just one example of how removing a binary, "either/or" framework in order to get to "Yes—and" allows for the type of creativity needed in addressing the challenges of extreme weather, social inequities, constrained access to resources, and the shifting social norms and expectations coming from the next generation of employees and customers.

"Yes—and" transcends departments, functions, situations, and even cultures. Both words have meaning that creates openness and curiosity, to opportunity, to challenges, to requests. "And" contains the power of inclusion, of connection, of non-duality. When they are used together, they serve as the cornerstone of communication and an essential element for brainstorming.

"Yes—and" is a tool for strengthening communication skills, staying engaged in the moment, leveling status, resolving conflicts, and creating a safe environment to share ideas, issues, and questions. So much of the dialogue around diversity, equity and inclusion or social justice, plus the complexities and trade-offs inherent in developing climate strategies requires an atmosphere of respect and safety so that ideas and responses can be raised. It takes the ecosystem of brands and commerce along with the public sector and community-based organizations as well as activists to address issues and responses from brands that can straddle the need for profitability with the tension of non-commercial commitments.

In this ecosystem of change, we need the activists who scream for our attention and keep challenging us. Who yell that the water is rising, that the climate is changing. I respect their voices and their passion. We will always need to hear how we need to move faster and do better. Also, there are a range of societal values and needs that can never be commercialized or made into a market. Health and well-being are not markets to exploit but human rights that can provide many with a good living but are not profit markets. Access to art and culture (museums, etc), access to the restorative powers of the out-doors and its beauty, cannot just be available as a market.

Lastly, we need governments and regulators. This last decade has shown the need for political will, democratic power, the preservation of rights, the need to set parameters and require certain adherence to protecting the public good. Guidance from the US Securities and Exchange Commission, formalized in May 2022, has been welcomed by many businesses who want to see guardrails established within which innovation and leadership can emerge (Newburger, 2022). And, those who are fast followers can also set a cadence and struc-ture for goals and metrics when it comes to climate mitigation, resil-ience, and adaptation.

All of this provides the opportunity for creativity and innovation in solutions that can address the challenges inherent in a company's efforts to manage its environmental and social footprint. Here are just a few of the new products, business models, and partnerships that are in development:

- Boston-based Mori has created a plastic-like food wrap made from natural silk protein. Applied in place of a thin plastic film or packaging, this biodegradable film slows down three key mechanisms that cause food to spoil. Mori is exploring how their nature-inspired innovation can provide protection for all kinds of foods, from produce to protein, while delivering a commercial solution that promises to double a product's shelf life.

- LiquidSpace is committed to developing and promoting solutions that support and accelerate the decarbonization of the workplace industry. One solution allows companies to hire out underused space in their offices—from desks to conference rooms to small meeting spaces—facilitating asset sharing for tens of thousands of partner locations in more than 2,000 cities.

- California-based Plenty is prototyping a two-acre farm that can produce 720 acres' worth of food. Their method utilizes machine learning and artificial intelligence to make sure the plants are getting all the light and water they need, ensuring that any type of fruit or vegetable can be grown all year round. Plenty's farms are designed to increase the yield of crops over 350x relative to traditional farming—a seriously promising technological solution for reducing greenhouse gas emissions while also feeding our growing population!

These examples speak to the need for sustainability leaders to be visible and lead in a "Yes—and" collaboration with designers, innovators, partners, and activists. Because we need everyone, everywhere, reinventing everything.

References

Aquilina, T (2021) Hasbro rebrands Potato Head toys with gender-neutral name, Entertainment, https://ew.com/movies/hasbro-rebrands-potato-head-with-gender-neutral-name/ (archived at https://perma.cc/S6VN-SUFA)

Boone, E H (2018) Research and collaboration put a tobacco-free generation within reach, *Stanford Social Innovation Review*, https://doi.org/10.48558/C4D5-0863 (archived at https://perma.cc/4RD6-DJG8)

CARE (2019) *Annual Report*, CARE, https://carpetrecovery.org/wp-content/uploads/2020/06/CARE-2019-Annual-Report-6-7-20-FINAL-002.pdf (archived at https://perma.cc/XP6U-LDYY)

Carmichael, M. (2022) What the future: Identity, Ipsos, www.ipsos.com/en-us/knowledge/society/What-the-Future-Identity (archived at https://perma.cc/JP7L-B3E9)

Colgate (2022) Colgate launches its groundbreaking recyclable toothpaste tube with 'Recycle Me!' packaging in the US, Colgate, www.colgatepalmolive.com/en-us/who-we-are/stories/recyclable-toothpaste-tube-recycle-me-packaging-us (archived at https://perma.cc/9JGP-48BS)

Forti, V, Baldé, C P, Kuehr, R, Bel, G, et al. (2020) *The Global E-Waste Monitor 2020: Quantities, flows, and the circular economy potential*, UNU/UNITAR and ITU, https://ewastemonitor.info/wp-content/uploads/2020/11/GEM_2020_def_july1_low.pdf (archived at https://perma.cc/H8NX-VHR4)

Heil, E (2019) The key to White Claw's surging popularity: Marketing to a post-gender world, *Washington Post*, www.washingtonpost.com/news/voraciously/wp/2019/09/10/the-key-to-white-claws-surging-popularity-marketing-to-a-post-gender-world (archived at https://perma.cc/V79P-Z9YM)

Irregular Labs (2019) The Irregular Report: Gender, activism, and Gen Z, Irregular Labs, https://medium.com/irregular-labs/the-irregular-report-gender-activism-and-gen-z-f8728212ef19 (archived at https://perma.cc/C4QX-5C84)

Japsen, B (2014) CVS stops tobacco sales today, changes name to reflect new era, Forbes, www.forbes.com/sites/brucejapsen/2014/09/03/cvs-stops-tobacco-sales-today-changes-name-to-reflect-new-era (archived at https://perma.cc/W5MJ-46U4)

Larson, J and Venkova, S (2014) Plastic bag bans spreading in the United States, Earth Policy Institute, www.earth-policy.org/mobile/releases/update122 (archived at https://perma.cc/2RPL-NKX3)

Leiva, L (2018) Meet Fluide, the makeup brand that believes in the power of inclusion—not tokenism, Allure, www.allure.com/story/fluide-the-new-makeup-brand-putting-representation-first (archived at https://perma.cc/CU4X-LCXY)

Mattress Recycling Council (2022) Retailer take back, Mattress Recycling Council, https://mattressrecyclingcouncil.org/retailer-take-back (archived at https://perma.cc/N9AU-ESGD)

Newburger, E (2022) SEC unveils rules to prevent misleading claims and enhance disclosures by ESG funds, CNBC, www.cnbc.com/2022/05/25/sec-unveils-rules-to-prevent-misleading-claims-by-esg-funds-.html (archived at https://perma.cc/KY7A-M3V4)

OECD (2001) *Extended Producer Responsibility: A guidance manual for governments*, OECD, https://doi.org/10.1787/9789264189867-en (archived at https://perma.cc/4AFE-FPB9)

OECD (2022) How we work, OECD, www.oecd.org/about/how-we-work (archived at https://perma.cc/JQ2U-LDZA)

PaintCare (2022) Our story, PaintCare, www.paintcare.org/our-story (archived at https://perma.cc/27R2-62ZW)

Porter Novelli (2021) 2021 Porter Novelli focus: All gender, Porter Novelli, www.porternovelli.com/findings/2021-porter-novelli-focus-all-gender (archived at https://perma.cc/C4TC-SKRY)

Reimagine Gender (2022) Understanding gender, Reimagine Gender, www.reimaginegender.org/understanding-gender (archived at https://perma.cc/GX84-7GC2)

Rubak, B (2022) Aldi, Wegmans and other grocery stores are expanding the ban on this item, Eat This Not That! www.eatthis.com/news-aldi-wegmans-other-grocery-stores-plastic-bag-ban (archived at https://perma.cc/DRS9-NWRN)

Siegel, T (2017) Hasbro CEO on "Transformers" future and marketing "My Little Pony" to boys, The Hollywood Reporter, www.hollywoodreporter.com/movies/movie-news/hasbro-ceo-transformers-future-marketing-my-little-pony-boys-1012852 (archived at https://perma.cc/E82M-VXF5)

Tallo (2020) The survey is in: Gen Z demands diversity and inclusion strategy, Tallo, https://tallo.com/blog/genz-demands-diversity-inclusion-strategy (archived at https://perma.cc/5TQV-WVGS)

WBCSD (2018) Design for disassembly/deconstruction, World Business Council for Sustainable Development, www.ceguide.org/Strategies-and-examples/Design/Design-for-disassembly-deconstruction (archived at https://perma.cc/77VU-9ZR6)

Dismantling Through Creative Destruction

06

Intentional Deconstruction Makes Room for Innovation

Purposeful brands have embedded throughout their organization the greater good they want to create in the world. They can answer the question, "What would be missing in the world if our company was not here?" They have made significant sustainability commitments, allocated resources, and are driving environmental and social innovation across operational processes as well as into new products and services.

In the process of operationalizing purpose, many are also coming face-to-face with the reality that some of their flagship products, systems, and business models are no longer useful. In fact, these established and successful systems may be preventing the deployment of the new products, processes, and solutions needed to protect planetary resources or ensure a strong social fabric. As the world inevitably shifts in this waking up, climate crisis, human reckoning moment, a corporation can change itself, be forced to change reactively, or cease to exist.

The concept of creative destruction was first described in 1934 by Joseph Schumpeter in *The Theory of Economic Development*. While most twentieth century economists focused on competition, Schumpeter insisted that disequilibrium was the driving force of capitalism. What he described was how, in times of disequilibrium, innovators and organizations with strong adaptation skills were better able to thrive during periods of rapid change. Those whose momentum and success were deeply entrenched in the status quo made the mistake of working to preserve rather than adapt.

We are living in a sea change of disequilibrium now as the realities of our Anthropocene Epoch are upon us (National Geographic, 2022). That is, this current geological age, which is seen as the period during which human activity has been the dominant influence on climate and the environment. The word Anthropocene is derived from the Greek words *anthropo*, for "man," and *cene* for "new," coined and made popular by chemist Paul Crutzen and biologist Eugene Stoermer in 2000 (Crutzen and Stoermer, 2010).

We are living through a shift from a fossil fuel economy to a decarbonized, net-zero economy. This disequilibrium is profound and accelerating, having a significant impact on brands. For companies to maintain their social license to operate, their stakeholders now expect them to participate in solutions that ensure a thriving planet and a fair society. Companies that ignore or dismiss ESG, sustainability, and DEI as passing fads will not be here by 2050. During periods of dramatic change, we have seen brands that have not successfully adapted. Where are the manufacturers of whale oil lamps, horse carriages, vacuum tubes, and steam engines?

Established brands no longer with us either dismissed or significantly discounted the signals of how new systems or technologies were going to affect their business, in some cases not only ignoring the shifts but deliberately becoming more committed to their existing products and core markets. The only way to avoid extinction is by staying curious, adaptive, and willing to partner or collaborate with new entrants.

Creative destruction is all around us and is now a key premise in multinational initiatives from NGOs like the United Nations, COP, and the Marrakesh Partnership—all global leaders in addressing climate change. Their new 2030 Breakthroughs, a January 2021 update to The Race to Zero Breakthroughs, sets out the specific, near-term tipping points for more than 20 sectors that make up the global economy (UNFCC, 2021). This blueprint is a master plan around which business, governments, and civil society must work, and by when, to deliver the sectoral changes needed to achieve a resilient, zero carbon future by 2050 at the latest.

The signals of where creative destruction is looming for companies are on every page of that report. A 2022 analysis by McKinsey spells out what it will take to create the net-zero economy envisioned by NGOs. To achieve net-zero emissions by 2050, McKinsey estimates that average annual spending on energy, mobility, industry, buildings, agriculture, forestry, and other land use will need to be $9.2 trillion. The effects on existing industry and infrastructure are profound. The implications to how society will adapt are also hidden in those numbers.

The United Nations is working to accelerate systems change so that new approaches can emerge to replace those no longer useful as part of its Race to Zero and 2030 Breakthroughs initiatives. In the transition to a decarbonized economy, the UN recognizes that to achieve net-zero, 20 percent of key leaders within each of the 30 sectors that make up the global economy must commit to playing their part in transforming themselves and their sector. These focused Breakthrough Initiatives are derived from the UN's Climate Action Pathways—a set of comprehensive roadmaps to achieve the Paris Agreement in line with 1.5°C across all sectors, developed by the UN High-Level Champions and the Marrakech Partnership—a vast coalition from across the climate action ecosystem.

What I found most interesting about the way in which the UN is framing the Breakthrough Initiatives is a comparison to other well know accelerations that have occurred as part of every major industrial disruption—the exponential change curve.

History is full of creative destruction and exponential change examples as technologies and new markets emerge. Those easiest to see looking back are that of the automobile and color TVs. Generally, disruptive solutions scale from minimal market share to over 80 percent share within an average of 10–15 years (UNFCC, 2021). If we think about more sustainable examples, renewable energy is another case study. In 2014, just one year before the Paris Agreement, electricity from sustainable sources such as solar and wind was only cheaper than new coal or gas plants in a small minority of countries around the world. However, according to the UN, "Today, in 2021, solar and wind are the cheapest form of new generation in countries covering over 70 percent of global GDP" (UNFCC, 2021).

The uptake of a new technology and the creation of a new market begin small initially, with growth appearing minimal, for example only 1 or 2 percent each year. However, what people often miss when looking at these numbers is that while the percentage size is small the rate is likely doubling, meaning that the transformation is happening exponentially. Market share numbers may be at 1 percent, growing to 2 percent; it quickly goes to 4 percent then 8 percent, to 16 percent, to 32 percent and so on as use of the technology moves from early adopters to more mainstream users. This is often a result of more of the market overcoming obstacles such as technological issues that might have been experienced by the early adopters.

When you dig into how this exponential change happens, a pattern is clear. Renewable energy, specifically solar, is a great example. As solar technology was being developed, costs were high, reliability and efficacy were uncertain. Solar panels were expensive, bulky, and did not generate reliable or significant amounts of electricity. During the decades of a learning and innovation curve, you begin to see an acceleration as improvements and efficiencies start to gain critical mass and generate what is also known as a flywheel effect—small wins that build on each other over time and eventually gain so much momentum that growth almost seems to happen by itself.

What happens next is that complementary infrastructure and ancillary products and services begin to emerge, and the technology enters its diffusion phase. In the case of solar, this is when you see solar installers and community-based aggregators and other players enter the space. Positive feedback and product uptake raises confidence and creates the buzz and momentum needed to draw in other players and adjacent sectors who begin developing add-on products and services. Household battery systems is a good example in residential solar (UNFCC, 2021).

Two clear examples of creative destruction are the emergence of a circular economy and the transition away from internal combustion engines in the automotive industry.

The emergence of a circular economy means moving away from the linear take, make, waste processes which are the legacy infrastructure of almost all commercial manufacturing today. It requires the creation of systems, processes, labor pools and the job skills needed to redesign products and manufacturing processes that reuse material that is the waste or byproduct of another system.

The circular economy takes a systems design approach and is based on three principles: (1) eliminate waste and pollution, (2) circulate products and materials at their highest use and value, (3) regenerate nature and intentionally improve ecosystems. A circular economy implies the transition to renewable energy and materials, decoupling economic activity from the consumption of finite resources. It also contains a commitment to doing so in a way that protects human wellbeing.

The Ellen MacArthur Foundation is the leading NGO working on creating a circular economy through partnerships with global brands, governments, academia and think tanks. Their description of the two components of circularity help define how this new economy is vastly different from the linear take-make-waste system that dominates today's world:

> Here are two main cycles—the technical cycle and the biological cycle. In the technical cycle, products and materials are kept in circulation through processes such as reuse, repair, remanufacture and recycling. In the biological cycle, the nutrients from biodegradable materials are returned to the Earth to regenerate nature.
>
> (Ellen MacArthur Foundation, 2022)

The implications for creative destruction and the need for radical adaptivity in reimagining systems can seem overwhelming. To move to a circular economy, we need new system thinkers who design products to be easily disassembled and the parts put back into the technical cycle as raw material for someone else's manufacturing process. Disassembly for recycling is good, but the better design outcome is to design for a circular economy. This means we need product and design methodologies that, rather than optimize for disassembly and recycle, provide a means for products to be reused over and over before disassembly. This is because the environmental impacts of reuse rather than single use represent the highest use value—one of the tenets of circularity. And this is just in the technical cycle.

For the biological cycle, we need to reengineer our waste systems so that we are putting food waste, agricultural byproducts, and even human waste safely back into the earth to recapture micronutrients and restore soil health. As part of industrialization, we've separated extraction from restoration and are simply extracting and then making piles of waste composed of technical and biological byproducts. For the biologic cycle, we can mimic nature and create systems and other agents—like mycelium (fungus)—to help regenerate and restore.

The apparel industry is an example of how complex this system is, since it is a combination of both technical and biological systems. Cotton, linen, and wool are all natural products. Rayon is a semisynthetic fiber, made from natural sources of regenerated cellulose, such as wood and related agricultural products. Polyester is a synthetic thread, created from petroleum products. The entire sector is a combination of both cycles. So, one of the first steps in thinking from a circular perspective is to find ways of keeping clothes in use.

Fashionable Changes

The apparel sector is one industry that has been experimenting with a range of circular economy concepts while simultaneously exploring how to move away from the negative environmental and social impacts of the fast fashion approach they introduced decades ago. Brands like Zara, Old Navy, Forever21, and H&M expanded fast fashion globally, by replicating high-fashion designs, mass-producing them at a low cost, and bringing them to retail stores quickly. These brands and the entire sector are in decline, according to a 2021 UBS investment bank forecast report on emerging trends in the fashion industry. The backlash is coming from customers who have learned what significant environmental damage is being done by creating throwaway clothes. The human dimension is also now visible to consumers who understand that an eight-dollar t-shirt depends upon sweatshop labor (Bain, 2021).

Dana Thomas, author of the 2019 book *Fashionopolis: The prices of fast fashion and the future of clothes*, describes what the apparel industry could look like if it worked through many of the challenges created by fast fashion:

> I would not be visiting some of those sweatshops that I saw in Bangladesh and Vietnam, which were just appalling. And I wouldn't be going to see dead rivers filled with runoff from jeans-washing factories in Ho Chi Minh that made me want to vomit. There would be fish in that stream. You wouldn't have bedridden 26-year-olds who can't have children because a factory collapsed on them. You wouldn't have landfills full of clothes. You'd have more fields of indigo and organic cotton.
>
> (Chua, 2019)

A few innovators are showing up and challenging the status quo in the apparel industry, some are even partnering with big established brands who are embracing creative destruction through collaboration.

If the trend is away from cheaply made, almost disposable clothing, what is the opposite of that? There can be two solutions that address negative impacts. One is to create items that last. With design that is enduring rather than trendy. Made with materials that are durable and repairable. Clothing that can be cleaned repeatedly and not fall apart. Apparel that is noted for its classic design and is made to be passed on to others.

The second trend, which actually depends upon the first (greater durability in clothing), is to share, rent, and recirculate items worn for a time and then returned.

ThredUP, founded in 2009, is a managed marketplace that buys and sells secondhand clothes in an ever-expanding network of partners and collaborators. According to their website, they are a "circular closet, powered by proprietary technology" (ThredUP, 2022a). They accept, process and recirculate over a hundred thousand items a day, have more that two million items listed on their online store and handle over five million pieces of clothing in their distribution centers, on their way from someone's closet to someone else's. In 2022, ThredUP released a resale report that placed the resale market at $9 billion and projected it to increase to more than $47 billion by 2025. According to ThredUP, that rapid increase in projected growth is driven by more sellers putting products into the market that are highly sought by resale consumers. Between 2000 and 2015, the number of items of clothing sold each year more than doubled to about 100 billion units. A new industry and a new marketplace are emerging before our eyes (ThredUP, 2022b).

The ThredUP marketplace functions as a business to consumer model, working directly with individuals who want to either sell their own clothes or purchase previously worn items. Customers who want to sell their clothes get a free "Clean Out Kit" with a prepaid label to ThredUP. When the company receives the items, they are sorted and processes them for resell which includes photographing, evaluating, and valuing each garment. Sellers can get cash payment for their items, get online credit, partner credit, or make a charitable donation. Items that do not meet the company's 12-point inspection process and are listed in the marketplace, go to secondhand clothing shops (thrift stores) and textile recyclers.

It's the partnership with key apparel brands that makes ThredUP's approach game changing. As fashion brands look to move away from fast fashion and enhance customer loyalty, many have looked to return and resale as part of their omnichannel strategy. But most retailers don't have the infrastructure to receive used items, process and resell them. They do, however, have a keen interest in making sure any item that has their name or logo on it does not end up in a landfill or be seen as part of the negative story inherent in clothing waste.

Enter ThredUP. They have created a business-to-business solution, resale-as-a-service (RaaS) that allows brands and retailers to leverage the ThredUP technology platform and distribution channels. Brands provide Clean Out Kits on their own commerce to customers who can send used clothes from any brand to ThredUP and get paid in branded-store credit like gift cards. Retailers win new customers and encourage customer loyalty by offering vouchers through Clean Out Kits in partnership with ThredUP, attracting younger demographics with lower price points and increasing store or site traffic with the ability to constantly update their inventory and offer new (resale) products.

And it's working. ThredUP posted revenues of $186 million in 2020, a significant jump from 2018's $129 million (Market Watch, 2020).

Resale, rent, buy less, repair, personalize, and redesign are all trends emerging in the fashion sector. Patagonia will take any of its items for repair, either at the store if it's a small tear or missing item or send to its Reno Nevada location for more comprehensive fixes (Patagonia, 2022).

More than ten years ago at a sustainability conference, I remember hearing a speaker from one of the major jeans brands talk about the future of clothing retail stores and the image he described has stayed with me. He speculated that, as more and more people came to understand that throwaway clothing was not good for people or the planet, they would be looking for clothes that lasted longer and could still express their unique personal style or a new design trend. So he encouraged fashion brands to begin thinking about creating retail stores that offered three distinct experiences. He imagined that a third of the store would showcase new items by offering a range of sizes that could be tried on but would then be shipped to the customer's home rather than needing to keep so much inventory on the floor. Think of these more as "showroom" sections in the clothing store. The next section of the store would feature resale items. And the last third would be a repair/creative space where customers could bring in their clothes and sew on a button or fix an unraveling hem. Or, using fabric swatches and other accessory items provided by the brand, take their own clothes or maybe a reused item they've just purchased, and turn it into a one-of-kind jacket, dress, or trouser.

I still love this idea. The concept works on so many levels. It takes floor space and, rather than simply being a way to manage inventory, you're creating a space for community gathering. You're reusing buttons and bits, scraps, and other "waste" items to create something entirely unique and new. You are giving your customers a way to remain loyal to your brand, even as they and the world around them change and evolve.

Circular economy is one instance where creative destruction shows up to replace a system like take-make-waste and replace it with a new way of doing things. Sometimes creative destruction is the literal shutting down of product lines and companies who fail to make a disequilibrium pivot. We are living through such an era when it comes to transportation and the move shift from motors to mobility.

From ICE to BEV

The internal combustion engine (ICE) is dying. Like the dinosaurs whose petroleum-based remains have been fueling them for over 150 years, automobiles, trucks, and buses are in the midst of a worldwide transformation. The ICE is becoming the battery electric vehicle (BEV). Taking a closer look at the automotive brands who are knee deep in this transition is to get a front-row seat in creative destruction.

In order to achieve the kind of emissions reductions significant enough to limit climate change will require that the current economy both rapidly phase out emitting vehicle sales and significantly accelerate fleet turnover, according to Emil Dimanchev, author of the 2022 book *The 4Ds of Energy Transition: Decarbonization, decentralization, decreasing use and digitalization.* To limit global warming to 1.5 degrees Celsius—a goal in line with the Paris Climate Accord—sales of internal combustion vehicles have to start phasing out in 2025, but the lifespan of those vehicles will also have to be reduced from 16 years (the current average in the United States) to nine years.

These facts raise interesting questions. Should automakers give their current gasoline and diesel cars shorter lifespans, so they only last until their BEV lines are at full production capability? The problem with this approach is the inherent waste of ICE vehicles designed for obsolescence. That would be a throwback to the heyday of the auto industry in the 1950s, when buyers were encouraged to trade in their cars annually to get the latest styling changes like swooping fins and chrome grills. Or, could automakers develop trade-in and refurbishment programs that convert gasoline-powered vehicles into battery-powered vehicles?

This is also a place for partnerships and policy moves, encouraged by automakers, in addressing the need for a rapid transition. Perhaps there should be statewide incentives that focus on retiring ICE vehicles rather than buying new BEVs. This is not a new concept. The 2009 Cash for Clunkers was a US government program that provided financial incentives to car owners to trade in their old, less fuel-efficient vehicles for more fuel-efficient ones.

The most important difference between ICEs and BEVs from a manufacturing perspective is the replacement of the traditional engine with an electric motor. This frees automakers from the complex and labor-intensive assembly of ICEs and allows them to focus instead on relatively simple electric motors. This is a significant change for an industry that has spent more than 100 years developing and improving engine manufacturing and vehicle assembly to the highest degrees of efficiency.

This massive system shift from ICE vehicles and gas stations to BEVs and charging stations involves a complex set of stakeholders and participants well beyond automaker.

The challenge facing the auto sector is how legacy auto brands can differentiate themselves from others in an exploding EV market. Like all previous sector transitions, such as the airline industry expansion in the 1960s, the debut and proliferation of personal computers in the 1980s, and the vast iPhone apps marketplace in the 2000s, there is a rush to create products and rapidly seize market share.

Several automobile manufacturers have made pledges to either stop or drastically reduce producing cars with internal combustion engines between 2030 and 2035. Audi, a subsidiary of Germany's Volkswagen, pledged to launch only fully electric vehicles starting in 2026 and quit making ICE cars by 2033. General Motors said it plans to stop building polluting vehicles by 2035 but has not explicitly stated if or when it might offer only electric vehicles (FirstPost, 2021).

Today, what's different is that this EV market shift is responding to an existential climate crisis that more and more people are acknowledging. And we lack the language and consistent parameters for deciding how we as consumers should enter this market, what to expect, and how the act of transitioning from ICE to BEV helps mitigate climate risk.

According to Porter Novelli research, there is massive confusion about impacts and effects—there is no set terminology (zero emissions, circular, etc.). And other research tells us that consumers are looking to brands to lead on climate (more than they expect governments or NGOs) while also expecting those brands to help their customers live more sustainable lives (Porter Novelli, 2021).

Purposeful auto brands will be the ones who understand that behavior change is hard. Social change is hard. They will bring the buyer along that change journey, making it easier in as many places as possible. This requires thinking through and taking ownership of parts of the system change to reduce transition friction. This can include helping customers get rid of their ICE vehicles to buy a BEV through a new type of trade-in program. Or making the installation of a home charging station part of the deal. Or working with local communities to accelerate the build out of a charging system. Or creating BEV rideshare pools to bring EV use to a wider range of people, including those who don't want to or can't own their own car.

This points to an emerging challenge that is rising to the top—the question of equity in the emerging BEV market. In the United States, both the Department of Transportation and the Department of Energy are looking at how to build this new transportation infrastructure without leaving certain communities behind. The goal is to not create electric charging deserts in poor communities and to work with automakers to ensure they include lower price BEVs that are accessible to people with many different income levels.

Automakers have an opportunity to lean into equity here and bring an equity mindset to product development, figuring out how to design and build a BEV for every budget. EV ownership is not practical for every underserved community because mobility needs of communities vary. Poor rural communities rely more on vehicle ownership or informal ride-sharing because of bad public transportation services and access. Poor urban communities in densely populated cities may have less of a need to own a car to get to work or complete daily tasks.

Partnering with community-based organizations should be a first step for automakers looking to create EV projects in underserved communities. Together they can gather relevant information in a culturally appropriate way (e.g., literacy level, language access, cultural issues/attitudes). An example of how this could work is to do a community mobility needs assessments while working to determine where charging stations could be sited.

Sacred Cows and the Status Quo

Inertia is a powerful force. The challenge in deploying a creative destruction strategy is how much resistance there will be from many parts of the organization. A purposeful brand challenges many of the sacred cows of capitalism and commercial success. Its very existence is based on the premise that stakeholders beyond just shareholders matter in any consideration given to strategy, growth, resource allocation, and outcomes. One of the most cited push backs to purpose has been that it gets in the way of what businesses are supposed to do, according to Milton Friedman's admonition to make as much money as possible while conforming to the basic rules of the society.

The counter opinion to Friedman is a growing understanding that a business's social license to operate is much more nuanced and complex in today's rapidly changing world where social systems, hyper innovation cycles, cultural shifts and population growth are happening exponentially. The role that corporations and CEOs are expected to play now includes responsibility for more than just profit. The sacred cow of profit above all else is waning. But maintaining the status quo can still stall change agents.

The term "status quo bias" was first introduced by researchers William Samuelson and Richard Zeckhauser in 1988. In a series of controlled experiments, participants were asked a variety of questions in which they had to take the role of the decision-maker in situations faced by individuals or managers. The results revealed a strong status quo bias that showed, when making important choices, people are more likely to pick the option that maintains things as they are currently (Zeckhauser, 1988).

Fear and uncertainty are two of the most critical components of inertia and resistance to change. However, to lead in these changing times, it takes courage and the capacity to embrace the truth of what is broken, and pivot as fast as you can to redefine success—dismantling your current business model while simultaneously building a new one in its place.

References

Bain, M (2021) Could climate-conscious shoppers kill fast fashion? Quartz, https://qz.com/1995090/could-climate-conscious-shoppers-kill-fast-fashion (archived at https://perma.cc/Z8FJ-WLQH)

Chua, J M (2019) The environment and economy are paying the price for fast fashion—but there's hope, Vox, www.vox.com/2019/9/12/20860620/fast-fashion-zara-hm-forever-21-boohoo-environment-cost (archived at https://perma.cc/CZR2-DS7J)

Crutzen, P and Stoermer, E F (2010) Have we entered the "Anthropocene"? IGBP, www.igbp.net/news/opinion/opinion/haveweenteredtheanthropocene.5.d8b4c3c12bf3be638a8000578.html (archived at https://perma.cc/6UDJ-UFMV)

Ellen MacArthur Foundation (2022) What is a circular economy? Ellen MacArthur Foundation, https://ellenmacarthurfoundation.org/topics/circular-economy-introduction/overview (archived at https://perma.cc/9944-PKZ4)

FirstPost (2021) EVs are the future: A list of all carmakers who have decided to phase out ICE vehicles and go electric, Firstpost, www.firstpost.com/tech/auto-tech/evs-are-the-future-a-list-of-all-carmakers-who-have-decided-to-phase-out-ice-vehicles-and-go-electric-9744401.html (archived at https://perma.cc/G4V7-LA8X)

Market Watch (2020) ThredUP Inc, Marketwatch, www.marketwatch.com/investing/stock/tdup/financials (archived at https://perma.cc/9JUL-WJR3)

McKinsey (2022) The net-zero transition: What it would cost, what it could bring, McKinsey, www.mckinsey.com/capabilities/sustainability/our-insights/the-net-zero-transition-what-it-would-cost-what-it-could-bring (archived at https://perma.cc/3UXY-MF88)

National Geographic (2022) Anthropocene, National Geographic, https://education.nationalgeographic.org/resource/anthropocene (archived at https://perma.cc/5CLF-MD3V)

Patagonia (2022) Repair process, Patagonia, https://help.patagonia.com/s/article/Repair-Process (archived at https://perma.cc/7UWM-3ELJ)

Porter Novelli (2021) Introducing the Porter Novelli focus: Business action for climate crisis, PN, www.porternovelli.com/findings/introducing-the-porter-novelli-focus-business-action-for-climate-crisis (archived at https://perma.cc/TF4H-FMVB)

ThredUP (2022a) Our story, ThredUP, www.thredup.com/about (archived at https://perma.cc/G44R-4A9X)

ThredUP (2022b) 2022 resale report, ThredUP, www.thredup.com/resale (archived at https://perma.cc/2LW3-UL6C)

UBS (2021) Not so fast fashion: How do we slow down the fast fashion cycle? UBS, www.ubs.com/global/en/investment-bank/in-focus/2021/not-so-fast-fashion.html (archived at https://perma.cc/C827-8FQW)

UNFCC (2021) *Upgrading Our Systems Together: A global challenge to accelerate sector breakthroughs for COP26 – and beyond*, United Nations Framework Convention on Climate Change, https://racetozero.unfccc.int/wp-content/uploads/2021/09/2030-breakthroughs-upgrading-our-systems-together.pdf (archived at https://perma.cc/HS3N-MCY3)

Zeckhauser, S W (1988) Status quo bias in decision making, *Journal of Risk and Uncertainty*, 1 (7), 59

Showing Up as Ally, Advocate or Activist

07

Purpose Requires a Backbone When Controversial Issues Arise

Employees, customers, investors, citizens—all these stakeholders' voices are getting louder, and their expectations from brands are increasing. For the first time, companies are being asked to engage with and positively impact outcomes that go far beyond delivering a profit or building an exceptional product. A wide range of stakeholders are now audiences whose influence forms cultural shifts in what to buy, what brands are relevant, what societal issues require response, and which corporate activities can drive cancellation.

A company's purpose, its North Star, is an expression of the greater good it wants to create in the world through the combined resources of its entire enterprise. Corporate purpose and business activism are rapidly evolving, driven in part by consumer and customer expectations for companies to show up in issues of social justice and play a part in fixing systems of injustice or participating in programs aimed at ensuring access to a healthy planet. The companies doing it right are focused on demonstrating an equal and meaningful commitment to all stakeholders.

Research conducted by Just Capital in 2022 showed that 92 percent of Americans overall (up from 79 percent in 2021) believe it is important for companies to promote racial diversity and equity in the workplace (Tonti, 2022). Additionally, across all demographics, Americans universally agreed that wages are key in doing so: 77 percent say that racial equity cannot be achieved without all workers being paid a living wage. These numbers expand on findings from an Ipsos study where consumers in the 18–34 age demographic ranked racial equality as one of their most important values (Garcia-Garcia et al, 2021). And a 2022 study from Deloitte found that Gen Z and Millennial workers who are satisfied with their employers' values, diversity initiatives, and societal impact are more likely to stay with that company for five or more years than those who are not (Deloitte, 2022).

Alan Murray, CEO of Fortune Media, former head of the Pew Research Center and author of the 2022 book *Tomorrow's Capitalist: My search for the soul of business*, has a good perspective on why the expectations on companies to participate in a wider societal fabric have changed so much. It's a perspective I've heard over the years as sustainability practitioners craft the "business case" for sustainability and attempt to explain why stakeholders beyond shareholders matter and issues beyond the boundaries of the company need to be considered:

> If you looked at the balance sheets of Fortune 500 companies 50 years ago, what you would see is that more than 80 percent of the value was physical stuff. It was plant equipment, oil in the ground, inventory on the shelves, all those things that you needed financial capital to build and that gave you value. You do the same exercise today and more than 85 percent of the value is intangibles. It's intellectual property, it's code, it's brand value. Those things are tied to people. So, I think the dynamics of business give people more power in the equation than they used to have.
>
> (Padhi, 2022)

This book is all about how a company can find and articulate its purpose, its North Star. There are many aspects to the process of finding and operationalizing purpose across the business—products, supply chains, sustainability, employee diversity, equity and inclusion.

An emerging aspect to purpose now includes wading into issues that have previously been seen as the sole purview of nonprofit organizations or activist groups. There were occasional flare ups of activism such as the 1980s withdrawal by Coca-Cola and others from South Africa in support of a wider anti-apartheid movement, but these were sporadic and rare. After the murder of George Floyd in 2020, followed by mass shootings and voter disenfranchisement, LGBTQ+ and gender identity controversies, women's health and abortion access, and the increase in extreme weather catastrophes, close scrutiny on how a company engages in both the dialogue and policies around these issues is now part of the public discourse and has become a tangible expectation of corporations and CEOs.

All of this leads to serious questions being asked in board rooms and on C-suite Zoom calls all over the world. How should we show up? What should our response be to this issue? How do we navigate the constantly shifting expectations of an increasingly vocal set of stakeholders? When do we have permission to participate? Is this too controversial for us if we engage? What if we don't?

The range of potential issues or crises is escalating. These can include episodes or patterns of violence or injustice towards specific communities (including but not limited to race, gender, religion, sexual orientation, gender identity, disabilities, etc.), or mass protests. They will also emerge when controversial state or national government actions impact specific communities (e.g., race, gender, religion, sexual orientation, gender identity, disabilities, political affiliation, etc.). Or when controversial acts by individuals, businesses or other corporate entities encroach on your company's territory. And the frequency of extreme weather events is leading to more and more natural disasters that inflict mass destruction and loss of life. Each of these can trigger an expectation that a brand take action or take a side.

For Sarah Ellis, the long-time president of GLAAD, it begins with Maslow's hierarchy of needs:

> If you look at Maslow, "safety" is foundational. So, the framework should be simple and factual: it's all about people's safety. Safety in schools, safety at work, safety for women, safety for the LGBTQ community. Safety for the under-represented. You're either for safety or against it.
>
> (Matlins, 2022)

I think that Ellis's summation is true on its face. Being *for* safety seems straightforward. But when you're the CEO of a public company, or the latest generational leader in a family-run business, balancing sometimes opposing business requirements and a wide range of opinions and beliefs is a profound challenge.

There are ways for determining when and how your company should show up when controversial issues arise. Many brands have developed an assessment process, as part of a comprehensive purpose implementation effort, that helps executives analyze and respond to controversies, issues, and crises as they arise. These frameworks also help guide ongoing communication and engagement around key issues, populations or geographies that have meaning to the company and its audiences.

In 2020 and 2021, we saw several companies begin posting social media content around Black History Month or Juneteenth. Unless these companies had been making progress on the operational dimensions of their internal DEI programs, such content was seen as performative at best and disrespectful and duplicitous at worst. As Just Capital research clearly shows, people expect companies to demonstrate a commitment to equity beginning with worker wages (Tonti, 2022). Pay equity across gender, race and ethnicity must be the priority when developing a response to incidents like racial protests or commemorations of key dates like the 1921 Tulsa race massacre or Abolition Day, which is celebrated on 1 August in many former European colonies around the world.

Both dimensions of support need to be in place. A brand needs to make sure its own house is in order, that it is carefully and systematically assessing its policies and programs and identifying areas for improvement when it comes to diverse representation and equitable treatment of workers. Only then can a company communicate support for or solidarity with milestone moments and commemoration days.

This doesn't mean that a company must have every dimension of its DEI program in place before speaking out. In fact, Porter Novelli research from 2021 indicates that 68 percent of Gen Z and 76 percent or the general population says that a company doesn't have to be perfect when talking about social justice issues, but it should be open and honest. That means, being transparent about progress against goals and speaking frankly about challenges or friction points companies might be facing when trying to meet goals. This is true for social issues as well as climate or environmental issues. People are looking to companies to be engaged in issues, be clear about what they are trying to accomplish, and provide regular and specific status reports on how it's going (Porter Novelli, 2021a).

As brands react to stakeholder expectations around engaging on social issues, many have begun talking about the processes they have put in place to help guide consideration, executive discussion, decision-making, and resource deployment when crises, issues or even a steady participation in cultural milestone moments (LGBTQ+ Pride, Black History, Earth Day). What companies are beginning to develop is a structure that allows for consistency and transparency about when and how the brand will engage on social issues, topics, and events.

As brands continue to define and refine their purpose, such a process that links the highest-order expression of purpose to individual events or incidents will need to be in place so that a company can ensure there is not a widening say/do gap. There will be times when an organization will be compelled to respond to significant social and cultural events and issues. This is not only because of how a brand expresses its purpose, but also because of how these situations impact employees, customers and their families, and the community at large.

Social issues can be defined as prevalent issues or opportunities affecting society that can generate intense or conflicting opinions based on what people believe is ethically correct or incorrect. When a high-profile incident, debate, or legislation related to a social issue occurs, brands are being called upon or feel obliged to act. Not only is there a range of issues that companies are being asked to engage in, but there is a spectrum of actions, interventions, programs, or commitments that can also be expected.

How is a company to make sense of the pressures that come when the hot spotlight of expectation shines on a company, its CEO or brand ambassadors to join, sign, engage, advance, or thwart social, political or cultural movements? Or support communities devastated by violence, inequity, extreme weather, or violence?

A helpful framework for understanding the matrixed realities of issues, relevance, urgency, and interconnected stakeholder needs is a continuum of personas that I have developed: ally, advocate, and activist. These three personas are a good way of categorizing the tenor and tone of a company's response as well as a way of describing the commitment and longevity of a brand's participation in a particular issue. Most companies will engage as all three, at different times and on different issues. Being an ally, advocate, or activist depends upon the issue itself. Sometimes, if the incident or social issue is tangential to the business or its core purpose, demonstrating allyship is all that is needed. Other times, critical issues are central to a business or its customers and activism is called for.

Even though these personas can look like a continuum, it is important to understand that it does not move along a good-better-best line. Allies are important elements of response and solutions to systemic problems. Advocates have a different role to play. And an activist is a visible and action-oriented approach that is best deployed against a handful of key situations. There are only a handful of brands we would consider to be activist to their core. Ben & Jerry's is one—a self-described activist company. As stated on its website in the social mission section, it aims "to operate the company in a way that actively recognizes the central role that business plays in society by initiating innovative ways to improve the quality of life locally, nationally, and internationally". The key word in that statement is "actively." When paired with an intention to initiate innovative ways that improve quality of life, you have a clear commitment that Ben & Jerry's will show up as an activist when it comes to social issues. Their list of cultural movements and challenges is long—voting rights, racial justice, LGBTQ+ rights, climate justice, campaign finance reform. They are living out their purpose and delivering on their belief that ice cream can change the world (Ben & Jerry's, 2022).

Not every company is a Ben & Jerry's. And yet, there are some brands who have been leading in environmental and social sustainability initiatives over the past two decades, which gives them an approach that can help assess response to incidents and issues. However, most companies are just beginning to wake up and realize that their social contract, their license to operate—which used to be simply "provide well-paying jobs"—is no longer sufficient. The cultural landscape is now in a state of flux. The pace of change is also accelerating. The players are constantly shifting.

Navigating brand-relevant, business-aligned, situation-appropriate engagement is possible. It requires that companies do the hard work of creating an issues engagement team, establishing a methodology for sensing and surfacing issues, consistently deploying a well-understood governance and decision-making process, and having a well-established set of people and funds ready to engage.

A company's issue response infrastructure can be applied against any issue, determine the level of engagement, and track the impact and effectiveness of each situation. It just takes time and commitment to the process.

Structure

When a company is ready to formalize its decision-making process for engaging on social issues, to replace what is generally an ad hoc, by-the-seat-of-your-pants reactive set of meetings and Zoom calls, they will need a formal framework that has process, governance, structure, and a team of people who, over time, develop a way of reviewing and assessing issues in a consistent manner. Key elements of the framework include a specific and designated issues engagement team (IET)—a system for taking in and tracking when issues are bubbling up among employees and beginning to get traction as an area, and when they might be expecting their employer to weigh in on or express support for or protest against. A standard process assessment regime is needed, one that includes a way to score and weigh the different dimensions of an issue and its impacts across the business. Lastly, a good framework will include policies or guidance on how to interface with similar efforts across business units or within and among various entities if the company has multiple divisions or operating units.

Team Roles and Responsibilities

Ideally, the team is composed of the highest-level executives in the company, specifically the C-suite: the president or CEO, the chief financial officer, general counsel, heads of human resources, corporate communications, marketing, and sales. Added to this group it is recommended that subject matter experts have a role in deliberation. These can include the sustainability lead, chief diversity officer or key employee resource groups with direct experience or insight into issues. This group should be composed of individuals who can bring the voices or perspectives of each key stakeholder group, serving as a proxy for representing how an issue or crisis is or might affect them. This must be done in balance with maintaining a strong sense of responsibility for the business and its commercial concerns. The tension between business objectives and the needs of the wider world or society become especially visible during the rise of a social issue or in the event of a catastrophe.

Consistency among the members is key. As companies are being pressured more and more to sign a letter, post on social media, or make a policy statement, it is helpful when the team has built a rapport and shared experience in how to learn, evaluate, and act—or not—in a stream of situations. I have found that once the engagement team has weathered a few of these deliberations, they develop a certain rhythm and begin to build confidence in their ability to thoughtfully navigate issues. Primarily they see that simply having a process and methodology through which to take a decision helps with any who may not agree with the outcome. The process and question filter can be refined over time, but the framework itself begins to create rigor and defensibility in how and why engagement decisions are made.

Issue Sensing and Surfacing

Almost every company has a social media presence consisting of company-generated content on platforms like LinkedIn, Twitter or TikTok. These platforms give brands a way to engage with consumers and other stakeholders as well as track how people are talking about the company. Monitoring media coverage, social media chatter, inbound customer complaints to call centers, regulatory inquiries are all sensing mechanisms which companies can use to monitor issues. Tracking former and current employee postings to job sites like Glassdoor is another way to surface criticism or causes that are evolving among the employee base. These should be monitored, in addition to annual employee surveys, to discover issues that may be bubbling below the surface.

Employees and customers are the two most important stakeholders whose concern about issues or requests for company intervention need to be carefully considered. Over and over during the summer of 2020 and the growing awareness of systemic racism with the rise of Black Lives Matter, company executives turned to their Black employee and diversity resource groups to listen and learn. Decisions taken to invest in anti-bias training, to support diverse suppliers, to rectify pay inequities, to support community organizations that address racism came from CEOs first listening to their Black employees and ensuring their perspectives were part of the solutions. This was usually followed by careful surveying of customer sentiment and consumer attitudes.

What consumers expect of companies has radically changed since 2019. Porter Novelli pulse research, fielded almost every quarter during 2019 and 2020, tracked how these sentiments changed in real time. In October of 2019, research showed that 90 percent of Gen Z believed companies must act to help social and environmental issues, with 75 percent saying they will do research to see if a company is being honest when it takes a stand on issues (Porter Novelli, 2019). By May of 2021, we saw that more than half (58 percent) of employees said that they held their employer to a higher standard than other companies when it comes to addressing social justice issues and 43 percent said they were reconsidering their current job because their company is not doing enough to address social justice issues externally (Porter Novelli, 2021b).

Having a means for sensing and surfacing the attitudes and sentiments of employees and customers, whether you are a consumer-facing brand or a business-to-business company, is a critical component of an issues engagement framework. Not all issues that bubble up will grow into areas that require some type of intervention. Sometimes, things flare and then die down because the matter has been handled well. Other times, external cultural forces and incidents continue to build, having a negative impact on both employees and customers. That's when a careful deliberation regarding engagement will be warranted.

One company I worked with about issue response had an interesting way of framing how to look at sensing and monitoring by establishing a threshold question that they also made part of their consideration. Their executive team had a session discussing hypothetical thresholds for various business indicators. If an issue began bubbling and a particular response was emerging, the timing of that response, that engagement, was also measured against certain business markers. For example, if one customer pulled its business contracts, that was not enough of a trendline to engage. But when either the contract size or a certain percentage of customers were expressing concern, the threshold was met and the time to engage was rationalized. They had the same discussion on share price elasticity as well as employee attitude scores. These business markers would be watched and, when nearing dangerous zones, action would be warranted.

Such an exercise in "what ifs" is an important element of planning. It helps develop a mindset that neither minimizes stakeholder reaction nor catastrophizes every flare-up as needing a full-throated response.

Decision-Making Methodology

For the decision-making process to be effective, it has to have a simple framework with a detailed set of questions that, ideally, are discussed and debated real time and then scored in a formula designed to weigh those aspects of the business that are most important or material.

At its core, a framework has five components.

1. Issue Assessment: Scope and Scale

The issue assessment is the listen-and-learn component. You are trying to answer the question, what do we know about what is happening? This is a critical phase that cannot be overlooked or given short shrift. A good technique, especially for those issues that have a political or divisive dimension, is to take a close look at the various positions surrounding an issue. Give two groups the task of researching, listening, and fact finding about both sides of an issue or controversy that your company is being asked to weigh in on. This gives you the broadest lens and helps ensure many diverse perspectives are considered. The assessment phase wants to uncover who the issue affects, if it is local or global, if it is part of a larger and more complex set of issues.

Right from the beginning, it is helpful to begin tracking the overall narratives associated with the issue, who the key players, spokespeople, messengers, and advocates are, and what they are saying. What storyline about the issue and its participants is already emerging will be an important consideration. Another data point will be a quick benchmark to see if your company's peers are already engaged, and if so in what way. Sometimes it becomes easier to show up in support of issues or policies if a critical mass of like companies or your customers and suppliers have already begun announcing their participation.

Lastly, this is the phase where additional information needed is surfaced. But resist the temptation to over-analyze and become paralyzed to taking a position or approving any action. In fast-moving, emotionally-charged times of crisis or culture change, it is important to remember that there will always be large gaps of unknowns. This is why the issues engagement team leans into the process, builds trust among themselves, and then makes the best decision they can, with the information at hand, grounded in an intention to do the right thing.

2. Values Alignment

Most companies have spent time and resources to articulate and continuously refine a set of values that provides employees, suppliers, partners, and customers with a set of guiding principles and fundamental beliefs that help them function together as a team and work toward a common business goal. Values are the "how" companies will show up, behave, and act. These can be a good place to check when determining when and how to join an emerging cultural movement or advocate for a social cause.

For example, if a brand expresses "Togetherness" as a corporate value, then assessing an issue which is creating divisiveness may be a place where that company could lean in and engage. Or, the value of togetherness may indicate that participating or showing up in response to a social issue will be most appropriate in concert with others. A value of togetherness can be achieved through a consortium or other collaborative solution. Alignment to corporate values is one of the first places where weighted scoring following a robust team discussion can begin to clarify possible responses.

3. Impact on Reputation

Determining the impact on reputation can seem like an ephemeral quest. Reputation is an intangible asset, part of what is now the largest segment of brand valuation. Research and insight teams at large brands and at brand strategy firms have sophisticated data research instruments and technology stacks that are constantly measuring and attempting to quantify the intangible value of a brand. Whether and how a company chooses to get involved with social issues can have a significant impact on reputation. So, how does the engagement team weight and score this dimension?

4. Business Relevance

Business relevance includes consideration and scoring of how a particular issue will impact the operational integrity of the company and its future revenue considerations. It starts with a look at how an issue might pose an immediate or direct threat to the safety, security, or wellbeing of employees. If not immediate, it is important to assess how not engaging might create a longer-term threat. The second set of questions will then expand an immediate and long-term threat consideration to next layer stakeholders like customers, suppliers, community members, and society or species at large.

This is also the place to identify if any stakeholder group has asked the company to participate. If pressure is coming from employees, investors, customers or suppliers, the business calculation on what impact either acting or not acting might have on those critical relationships needs to be thoroughly quantified. Lastly, from a historical perspective, it is important to identify if the company has previously taken a position on the emerging or aligned issues in the past. Such previous activity may be creating a sense of expectation from key players within the company and its orbit.

Another dimension of business relevance is to determine if engaging on the issue a company then creates opportunities for demonstrating alignment with its core offering or customer. It could be possible for the issue to provide an opportunity for the company to reiterate key values, reinforce (or share progress on) previous commitments, or provide an opportunity to take a leadership position or make a future commitment to an issue that is important to employees, customers, or within the broader industry sector.

5. Risk Assessment

The beauty of a clearly defined team, composed of leaders who serve as proxy for the widest range of stakeholders, is that risk assessment can be explored across a multi-dimensional consideration set. From the operational impact to supply chains, access to resources, or labor groups and employee cohorts, the viewpoint from chief operating officers and human resources executives can provide insight into both the tangible and human dimensions of an issue. Sales leads can provide insight to revenue impact. The questions across the business that can be asked to surface risk can include:

- What are our key customers saying, doing themselves, or expecting of us as it relates to this crisis or issue?
- Do our investors consider this an enterprise-level risk?
- Does participating, or not, impact business strategy or put revenue or market expansion at risk?
- How will our action or inaction affect our competitors, and our market share?

Governance and Resources

The issues engagement team should be formally established with its methodology and members transparently represented within the company. It is also a good idea to share the basic structure of the framework and its guiding principles with a range of stakeholders beyond employees. Shareholders and customers, suppliers and partners can all be briefed so that they understand, preemptively, how, and why a company will or won't respond to or express vocal alignment in times or issues flare-up. Transparency about who is making decisions, how those decisions are being made, how resources are allocated, are all part of good governance.

The same group should be present at all convenings and if someone cannot join, they should have a proxy join on their behalf. As needed, this group should also include experts and other impacted representatives in these conversations. During each discussion, someone should be assigned to take notes and provide a recap of decisions with the entire team, for transparency, documentation, and reference. These notes should be stored in a shareable and accessible format and location. Each issue discussion should follow the order of sections in the decision-making framework and may require the team to regroup as they gather more information, if needed.

Response Mechanism and Engagement Options

Once the team determines that an issue is important to the company and warrants some type of response, the options can seem overwhelming. The next section on personas will help refine the options but even before that classification is applied, some of the potential questions purposeful brands may ask themselves before they can show up as an ally, advocate or activist include:

- Will we speak out on the issue? If so, the company will need to designate a spokesperson or department who will own the development of a point of view.

- Is the audience internal, external or both?
- How will we support individual employee efforts (via donations, extra volunteer hours, awareness of work, etc.)?
- Who needs to approve this (HR, legal, finance)?
- Will we be reactive or proactive?
- Will we speak out independently, or in collaboration with partners, peers, industry groups, etc.?
- Who owns creation and approval of the messages, talking points, proof points and examples?

Guiding answers to the specifics inherent in the questions about should be clarity about what outcomes leadership is prioritizing. This can be an intention to show solidarity with, or support for, colleagues, partners, stakeholders, audiences, or an impacted community. It can also be to provide a unique, credible perspective and position on a situation, event or topic that is directly relevant to a company's expertise. Or, perhaps the brand simply wants to uplift existing expert voices, other brands or communities in the field who are commenting on a situation or playing in the specific space.

Often, taking on the role of convener or connector for communities, partners, stakeholders within a brand's specific sphere being impacted by the situation, event or issue is a strong role to take and one that can yield real world impact.

Engagement Personas

Now that we have explored the mechanics of an issues engagement framework and the various ways in which a response can be developed, let's take a closer look at the personas I mentioned earlier. Remember, every issue creates an opportunity to show as one of these three, or not at all.

Ally

To be an ally is an important role to play in times of crisis or shifting cultural or political discourse. Allyship takes a purposeful, thoughtful approach to showing up in community with those involved or affected. It implies that forming an intentional relationship, rooted in respect and empathy, is additive to those impacted or engaged in addressing issues or helping during a time of crisis. The overall approach of an ally is to learn all that the company can to determine how to best navigate situations or issues. Learning and listening are key components of being a good ally. Allyship starts with an empathetic posture of willingness and openness to other perspectives and leadership. If allyship seems like the right designation, it will be because the key motivation is to maintain a license to operate among communities or policy makers or avoid potential legal action.

The posture of an ally expresses or gives support to causes or groups. It is supportive but not directive or proactive. Allies are important because they begin to demonstrate critical mass behind an issue or an initiative. It literally is simply showing up and saying through participatory activities that "this is an issue of importance." This can include being a signatory to statements or joining as a member of supporting organizations. The pace of an ally is staying just behind cultural change. It is largely passive, measured, and the tone is supportive.

From a resource or asset perspective, the commitment to show up or participate in an issue stays both low commitment and low risk, allowing a company to engage with issues that are not core to the business or critical to some of your most closely held stakeholders.

When allies communicate about their involvement in an issue, it is largely to internal audiences like employees, suppliers, or partners. There can be some external communications like social media posts or website content or sustainability reports about efforts that demonstrate public support such as activities like donations, partnerships and appearances.

Advocate

The role of an advocate is to speak out on behalf of another or to publicly support and recommend a particular course of action or policy. It is more action-oriented than allyship, moving beyond an expression of support. Advocates lean in a bit more. Advocate for outcomes or commitments. Lend a voice for the voiceless. Are willing to speak on behalf of groups whose voices are not often heard. Or, perhaps more importantly, allow marginalized groups to leverage a brand's platforms to amplify other voices.

We certainly saw many examples of this in 2020 within the Black Lives Matter movement, when many celebrities and companies turned over their social media platforms to a wider range of voices who then had access to new audiences who could hear stories and experiences that came from those within communities of color. #SharetheMic was a global program, created by Bozoma Saint John, Luvvie Ajayi Jones, Glennon Doyle, and Stacey Bendet Eisner. According to their June 10, 2020 statement: "The campaign will be led by black women sharing their stories and experiences with the intention of forging essential relationships promoting activism in the entertainment industry."

When brands show up as advocates, they follow the first step of any issue engagement, which is to listen and learn. The nuanced difference of an advocate is that they take those learnings and apply them to their brand in an external and vocal way. The motivation for an advocate state is to send signals of support that strengthen relationships with customers, employees, and other mostly external stakeholders. The posture of an advocate is a champion of movements, campaigns, or policies that serve commercial and community interest. The advocate is aiming to change as culture changes, but they don't want to lead or provoke change. On issues that have a more direct impact on customers and employees, the advocate persona is a good way to show up with some clear intention to participate in solutions but not to lead on them. There is a mindset that commitments and resources deployed on these issues are a calculated risk that can potentially lead to a significant commercial upside.

When communicating their engagement on issues as an advocate, brands typically develop internal and external campaigns that many times are tied to products. These also warrant ongoing storytelling and data on the work in progress on how a brand is evolving internal structures to support the positive change for which it is advocating.

Activist

As we saw with Ben & Jerry's, activists lead by example to propel change. They come from a place of strong belief that some system or situation must change. That the status quo no longer works for them as a company but also no longer works for the wider society or planet. It's important to acknowledge that the activist persona on any issue is a rare occurrence among commercial organizations. The tension to deliver profit alongside managing social and environmental impacts is a tough path. Stepping out in front to lead, to agitate, to rally others adds a layer of complexity and scrutiny that can be difficult to navigate for many publicly traded companies. There are many companies that never show up as activists around social issues. Those that do will most commonly take on such a persona in reaction to a single issue or crisis that is materially linked to the company's business, profoundly relevant to most of its stakeholders, or is directly and negatively affecting customers or employees. It will always take the buy-in from the CEO and board of directors and involve engagement at the highest levels of leadership as well as employees across the organization.

The activist brand is motivated by almost a sense of calling to be true to what they believe and attract like-minded followers. Activists act—to drive change using their products, systems, infrastructure, and communities in an orchestrated approach to solving a macro problem or dismantling a destructive system. These brands are ready to be ahead of the cultural moment and have a bias toward action, often breaking new ground. They also often serve as a catalyst to motivate others. They sound bold, fearless, and provocative. Brands who show up as activists on a particular issue have a commitment to be a catalyst for change at all cost. Any significant commercial reward is often seen as a by-product and not a rationale for deciding to engage. Communication and campaigns articulate a vision for change and communicate bold first moves to lead progress and catalyze others to join. Campaigns are deployed to both internal and external audiences and are harmonized with other messaging and marketing efforts.

None of the Above

And let's not forget that sometimes the best response is no response. This consideration methodology can also create an outcome that indicates a wait-and-see approach is best. Not every crisis can warrant a mobilized response, especially as facts on the ground may not be fully known or motivations or those involved are not apparent. Which is not to say that sitting everything out is an option either. It is important to acknowledge that inaction or silence is, in fact, a response and will be perceived as an intentional decision to retreat from an issue.

The changing role of business in addressing social issues irrevocably changed when systemic racism became visible, or when the foundational structures of a functioning society were profoundly disrupted during the Covid-19 pandemic. Supply chains ceased working, and essential workers became the world's lifeline to healthcare and stocked grocery shelves or home delivery of everything. The role of business as an active participant in a well-functioning society or a thriving planet is now clear to many more stakeholders.

And these stakeholders are no longer silent.

Allstate Corporation's CEO Tom Wilson participated on a panel at the 2022 Aspen Ideas Festival, providing an overview of how his company makes decisions about where and how they chose to engage on environmental or social issues. He shared how their Societal Engagement Framework works and how it was created in response to the hundreds of requests they were receiving to sign onto issue letters. It starts with alignment to the company values. The second filter is "Does it help us do a better job for our customers?" The next question they ask themselves is whether they know anything about the issue, and if they have any agency or ability to affect solutions. The final question gets to what engagement on the issue means to their employees or if it has any impact on their reputation. From his perspective, such a framework is critical because, "if you stand for everything, then you stand for nothing" (Aspen Institute, 2022). According to Wilson, "Climate change and wildfires are right up our alley—it burns down our customers' houses, we know a lot about it. We can get things passed, and work with legislators and regulators to get that done." An interesting approach they took was to bring in some of their key investors to explain their methodology to inoculate them against investor concern. "We said, 'Hey, this is what we're doing, right?' So if somebody complains and wants to do a consumer boycott because we're not doing something about teaching standards in Florida, recognize it doesn't make it to our filters."

Milestone Moments and Cultural Celebrations

In addition to having a deliberate process and methodology for responding to inbound requests or crises as they are happening, many companies are also confronted with an increasing roster of cultural holidays and commemorations. How does a communications department decide when or if to create content as social feeds fill up with Earth images, rainbow flags, fists raised or flags flying?

As with crisis response, it starts with clarity on a company's purpose and values, and the realities of commitments, programs, and metrics already being tracked and communicated by the brand. From an environmental perspective, random Earth Day posts will ring hollow if there are no clear climate commitments and time-bound goals being met year-on-year. Equity and justice campaigns will be "purpose-washing" if companies do not have the internal mechanisms for addressing unequal pay, non-diverse leadership teams, or policies that perpetuate bias. Celebrating cultural anniversaries like Black History Month or Pride require an honest look at a company's say/do gap. Every company has such gaps. No brand can be on the leading edge of every issue that a wide range of stakeholders care about.

Participating in the social moment or engaging in the zeitgeist should align with company priorities. For some companies, its purpose will be mostly socially aligned. For others, it will be heavily invested in environmental impacts. That's the place to start when building an editorial calendar, marketing campaigns, and social media content. Is there a red thread of cohesion between who we say we are, what we have committed to accomplishing and where we show up with our voice? This becomes the primary filter for determining where to show up and how vocal to be.

Another element to bring into a communications campaign that celebrates or commemorates social issues is the voice of the community itself. From employee resource groups (ERGs) to customer affinity groups, brands have a wide range of people it can tap to participate in programs, initiatives, advertising, and philanthropic efforts. This is true across all of the myriad identities that each of us hold simultaneously. Gender, race, ethnicity, religion, political, disability, neuro differences all exist on a spectrum. Leveraging the diversity of lived experience, beliefs, perspectives, and creativity within each of these identities will help a company develop responses and engagements that ring true.

Once a milestone has been deemed relevant or meaningful, there are a range of options open to brands who want their calendar of activities and content to communicate progress on commitments. For example, in addition to building a stronger workforce, ERGs can also help to drive business and profits by providing consumer insights, fostering innovation, and broadening the corporate approach to social posts, advertising content or instore displays. Other activities can include inviting influential authors or activists to speak to employees about race relations, civil rights, or other critical topics surrounding identity. Or carbon emissions. Or environmental justice.

The key is alignment and a cohesive narrative that employees can embrace, customers can understand, and investors can make sense of alongside other business imperatives and risks. To stand for a few things that matter rather than a constant cascade of fleeting moments.

References

Aspen Institute (2022) Is trust the ultimate currency of stakeholder capitalism? YouTube, www.youtube.com/watch?v=qj9CItmedPk (archived at https://perma.cc/4XQ2-WEM6)

Ben & Jerry's (2022) Issues we care about, Ben & Jerry's, www.benjerry. com/values/issues-we-care-about (archived at https://perma.cc/HWP3-PXDL)

Deloitte (2022) The *Deloitte Global 2022 Gen Z and Millennial Survey*, Deloitte, www.deloitte.com/global/en/issues/work/genzmillennialsurvey. html (archived at https://perma.cc/ABG9-X24J)

Garcia-Garcia, M, Wahren, B, Midkiff, M and Espinosa, E (2021) *Forget Statements: Consumers want deeper social-justice commitments from brands*, Ipsos, www.ipsos.com/sites/default/files/ct/publication/ documents/2021-04/21-04-53_Forget_pov_v3.pdf (archived at https:// perma.cc/YPJ8-KPME)

Matlins, S (2022) A framework for CEOs and CMOs on when and how to enter the cultural conversation, Forbes, www.forbes.com/sites/ sethmatlins/2022/07/21/a-framework-for-ceos-and-cmos-on-when-and-how-to-enter-the-cultural-conversation (archived at https:// perma.cc/M2G7-TZW7)

Padhi, A (2022) Leadership rundown: Searching for the soul of business with Alan Murray, McKinsey, www.mckinsey.com/capabilities/strategy-and-corporate-finance/our-insights/the-strategy-and-corporate-finance-blog/leadership-rundown-searching-for-the-soul-of-business-with-alan-murray (archived at https://perma.cc/JEC3-VVE8)

Porter Novelli (2019) 2019 Gen Z purpose study: Undivided, Porter Novelli, www.porternovelli.com/findings/2019-gen-z-purpose-study-undivided (archived at https://perma.cc/XNG3-829P)

Porter Novelli (2021a) 2021 Porter Novelli focus: Gen Z and justice, PN, www.porternovelli.com/findings/2021-porter-novelli-focus-gen-z-justice (archived at https://perma.cc/9RFE-4B4B)

Porter Novelli (2021b) 2021 Porter Novelli business and social justice study, PN, www.porternovelli.com/findings/2021-porter-novelli-business-social-justice-study (archived at https://perma.cc/8G8B-MNKW)

Tonti, J (2022) Americans agree that advancing racial equity starts with paying a fair wage, Just Capital, https://justcapital.com/reports/ americans-agree-that-advancing-racial-equity-starts-with-paying-a-fair-wage (archived at https://perma.cc/Q9AY-YLJP)

Telling Your New Brand Story

08

Purpose and Sustainability Require a Communications Framework and Campaign Approach

Brands with a clearly articulated purpose that is operationalized across their value chain—from upstream to suppliers and downstream to customer use—need a narrative framework and communications platform capable of inspiring and informing.

Sustainability communications is complex and has evolved into two distinct areas. The first is finding a way to connect a brand's commitments and vision for its environmental and social initiatives to overall business strategy and brand value. The second requires an ongoing and precise communication of a company's ESG performance in alignment with stakeholder expectations. The evolving communications landscape requires integration across global corporate communications, marketing, sales, ESG reporting, investor relations, internal communications, and external employer brand efforts. This is because all these stakeholders are now looking for information about how a company and its products are either not harming the planet and people, or even better, contributing to improving impact.

What has proven effective for companies that are leading in sustainability strategy and ESG performance is a clearly articulated platform that captures how brand purpose is critical to business success and building long-term value. A crisp and clear expression of purpose strategy is the best way for a company to explain how it will account for and manage massive, paradigm-shifting externalities. This is now core to business communications and has emerged as a new specialty.

In fact, companies can expect an erosion of their social license to operate if they fail to take externalities into account in their core strategies and neglect to obtain insight into how externalities like climate change and cultural issues are affecting the business. Stakeholders have become increasingly savvy as to how business strategies may not be achievable at all if externalities are not included—and explained as part of an overall cadence of communications. All stakeholders want to understand that leadership is accounting for internal and external realities so that the business endures, with societal support, in a sustainable and environmentally viable way.

What Story Are We Trying to Tell?

The new brand story is rooted in double materiality. First, companies are being asked to understand and accommodate for the ways in which climate change and social issues are impacting their business. How are extreme weather events, raw material shortages, labor challenges due to environmental diaspora creating material risk in production or distribution? Most of the ESG data frameworks and ranking indices require specific information about a company's understanding of and plans for climate adaptation.

Second, companies must also report on how their business is impacting the climate and society at large. Operationally they are being held accountable for the emissions generated by the entire value chain of Scopes 1, 2 and 3. Scope 1 emissions are direct emissions from a company's owned operations, like factories, office buildings, distribution centers, and retail stores. Scope 2 emissions are the indirect emissions that comes from the power that a company purchases to run its operation, whether from coal-generated electricity from power plants or renewable energy from solar and wind. Scope 3 emissions are all indirect emissions that are not included in Scope 2 but are related to the emissions created by both upstream and downstream activities such as the emissions created when suppliers extract raw materials or consumers use the product in their daily lives (Greenhouse Gas Protocol, 2022).

Improving Scope 3 means working inside the company to change how products are made, used, and disposed of. It means understanding the need to reinvent consumer packaged goods like cleaners and detergents away from continuous consumption to refilling and durability. Many companies like J&J, P&G and Unilever are experimenting with refillable containers or cold-water detergent formulations to reduce Scope 3 emissions generated during consumer product use.

From a social perspective, companies are being held accountable to diversity, equity, and inclusion claims that they've made and are expected to provide ongoing reports about hiring practices, pay equity programs, worker safety and wellbeing, and even weigh in on issues like voting rights and access to reproductive healthcare.

All these externalities are part of a brand story—in varying detail, across a complex system of communications channels, and using a range of spokespeople. There is no one key message. There is simply too much complexity and mix of audience priorities for the sustainability narrative to be reduced to a single slogan or logo.

Organizational and Product Trust

People are reasonable. They know brands cannot solve every environmental and social issue at play in the world right now. But most people want to feel confident that the money they spend and companies they support reflect their values by engaging responsibly in the issues most pertinent to that brand or those products. This means making a commitment and bringing your customers into that story. Research shows that customers want to know what companies are doing at the product level and at the company level. According to research fielded by SB Brands for Good (2021), 85 percent of US consumers say they are loyal to brands that help them achieve a better and more balanced life.

The implication of this interest in both operational and product impact performance is that a sustainability narrative needs to express vision and progress at both the enterprise and product level. Brands need an ESG platform that can express the technical and complex environmental and social impact efforts happening across a company's owned operations and facilities as well as attributes being designed into products that lighten planet and people impacts.

One of the best ways for brands to build trust is to set an ambitious, big picture vision of what they want to achieve from an impact perspective and then show how it is supported by measurable goals and objectives. This is the same formula companies use to set financial performance goals against their long-term vision for growth and profitability. With a sustainability narrative, the opportunity is to connect the dots and integrate sustainability at the highest level of business strategy and embed it into the communications strategy as well.

A Sustainability Strategy Needs a Platform and Narrative Framework

From climate to diversity, from packaging and waste to labor to human rights, companies have a far-reaching set of activities that can have either positive or negative outcomes on the planet and society. A robust ESG/sustainability program has now been proven to be a consistent predictor of a well-run company—one that carefully manages its resources, reduces expensive waste, has minimal staff churn thanks to talent management and DEI programs that create a welcoming culture, and has the expansive policies, commitments, and organizational structure in place to ensure consistency in delivering strong ESG/sustainability results.

The components of ESG/sustainability communications are the same as any robust program. Best practice is to develop an ESG/sustainability platform that provides a cohesive wrapper and rationale to which the entire spectrum of environmental, social, and governance commitments and programs can be authentically linked and understood.

Communication is an integral and often overlooked component in ESG/sustainability. Think about it this way. Businesses are used to providing ongoing communications across owned, earned, and paid channels when it comes to business updates, product marketing, brand advertising. These communications campaigns deal with a specific range of business performance information. Yes, it includes investor relations and updates on financial performance as well as overall business health, risks, and opportunities. And marketing campaigns showcase information about products or services with a "why buy" message. What's been missing is a broad communications program that expands this language of business to include goals, progress, challenges, and anecdotes about the other components of how a company is operating across its entire ESG continuum.

There are a few key components to building an effective sustainability message platform. Ideally, these should be designed to last between five and ten years as they will be articulating a strategic vision tied to material, science-based goals. In most cases, the framework will be centered across several pillars, but articulate a vision that leans more heavily toward either an environmental or social set of commitments.

The sustainability narrative will integrate current sustainability commitments and goals, strategic pillars and targets, and allow room for individual brands to ladder up to it.

Step 1: Research and Insights

Great communications and messaging are grounded in facts and insights. The first step in developing a platform is to evaluate a company's sustainability commitments and communications, including existing programs, internal and external communications, and current business and product messaging and structure as it relates to any impact messaging or ESG attributes.

Another key component of research includes getting information and insights from stakeholder interviews across the enterprise, internally with departments like sustainability, marketing, communications and any assigned ESG integration responsibilities like operations, facilities, procurement, legal, HR, and sales. Engaging brand marketing and communications representatives in this process ensures framework alignment to brand and other communications articulations and lays the groundwork for future implementation and alignment.

An in-depth inventory of public-facing sustainability materials like sustainability reports, media coverage, press-releases, social media posts, or executive communications also helps provide insight into what has been said and how progress has been framed, and should reveal any strength or gaps.

Alongside the deep internal assessment, any good messaging framework needs some outside context against which to compare and contrast. This is best accomplished by benchmarking two to three best-in-class reporting brands to show leading sustainability narrative structure. It is important to compare similarly structured companies. For example, if your company has a "house of brands" structure with a range of individual brands that all ladder up to a single or different enterprise brand, it will be useful to see what others have done in similar situations. Some sustainability narratives have a very broad set of ambitions and goals at the enterprise level but then each of different product portfolios might be focused on delivering progress against different aspects of those goals. For example, a snack brand might concentrate on making progress on compostable packaging while a beverage brand might have a water reduction goal as its primary measurement for hitting a resource management goal.

Lastly, a scan of current sustainability landscape and trends to identify gaps and opportunities for sustainability communications and sustainability impact programming should factor in best practices, business alignment, cultural context, and sustainability impact opportunity that a framework could address.

Stage 2: Platform Ideation

To best drive alignment across the many silos where sustainability is being implemented, an ideation workshop is a smart initial aspect of Stage 2. After all the research, analysis and insight gathering are completed, gathering all those stakeholders who participated in the interview process to help sift through the results and prioritize the top two to three focus areas is a best practice I have deployed over the years.

Many companies will have a wide range of goals, metrics, programs, and outcomes that all fall under three or four pillars. These pillars can include product innovation, operational impacts, community and people, and philanthropy. Or they could include equity, climate, and ethics dimensions. The point is that each company will have a unique set of environmental, social and governance ambitions that align with the business—its strategy and structure. A sustainability framework needs to work with and extend how strategy and structure are experienced and expressed, when it comes to creating a greater good.

A working session with key internal stakeholders to develop and further refine corporate narrative for sustainability should result in:

- an architecture for organizing the sustainability programs, elements, and proof points
- direction for ways that those individual brands or initiatives plug in
- key messages that support the corporate sustainability architecture
- recommendations on how consistent messaging can be used across various channels

A robust sustainability platform is outlined in Figure 8.1.

Figure 8.1   Sustainability narrative platform, 2022

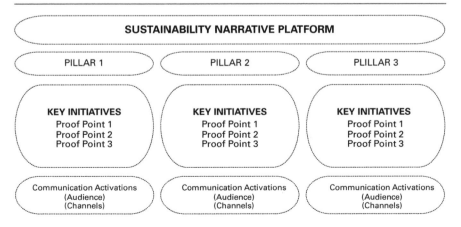

The Evolving Sustainability Report

An important output that will leverage the sustainability framework and narrative structure is the annual report. Over the years, it has been called a corporate social responsibility (CSR) report, an ESG report, a global impact report, and many other names that are either generic or might be specifically tied to a framework or campaign. It used to be a printed tome, until the environmental impacts of printing were compared to the benefits of an online document that could be printed at will were analyzed. Now these PDFs can range from 20 to 150 pages. Often the theme of the report will change every year, even if its overall category name remains the same.

We are seeing a clear evolution in both the use and form of the annual report and its connection to all the other types of sustainability data and storytelling that are needed throughout the year. What is emerging is a consensus that the annual sustainability report is evolving into several information streams that will be matched to the data and inspiration needs of employees, investors, customers, suppliers, procurement departments, regulators, partners, and activist groups.

An annual sustainability report is a moment-in-time look at specific updates on progress against time-bound goals. Two decades ago only a handful of companies published a sustainability report, but the Governance & Accountability Institute found that by 2011 approximately 20 percent of the largest 500 companies in the US published a sustainability report and by 2020 some 92 percent of the S&P 500 companies did so (Governance & Accountability Institute, 2021).

Over the years, these reports have gotten too big and bloated, and I'm not really sure who the audience is anymore. I expect to see both a shortening of reports for companies who migrate to scorecards or executive summaries. There will also be special white papers or issue reports that go deep in a particularly material area that has far-reaching implications to the company. There is a real opportunity to split out ESG data and sustainability strategy stories into multiple types of differentiated content.

In late 2022, I conducted a series of in-depth interviews with representatives from key stakeholders who use sustainability information as part of their consideration set when working with brands. I talked to investors and fund managers at Nasdaq and BlackRock. I interviewed an ESG corporate liaison from a global environmental nonprofit, and I talked with supply chain and procurement consultants responsible for driving ESG alignment across multiple sectors on behalf of global buyers.

Those interviews validated what I had begun seeing during sustainability report client projects. First, reports have gotten much too long and unwieldy. They were originally designed for two key reasons: (1) to provide technical information to a small group of specialists who understood the environmental dimensions of what was being reported; and (2) to tell a handful of stories and anecdotes that drove brand or reputational value in a few innovative ways. From the beginning, sustainability data has been voluntarily reported by companies who wanted to get credit for the investments they were making in emissions reductions or efficiencies that were also delivering financial or other benefits. And, in the absence of any leading rigorous frameworks that contextualized this information and stories, companies could cherry-pick the best results, the most interesting examples happening on the ground.

Fast forward to the present, and now several realities have emerged that are changing the way companies report their sustainability commitments, progress, investments, and challenges. There are now a handful of frameworks or ranking indices that have become de facto standards—TCFD, MSCI, and SustainAlytics are most cited as the best and most comprehensive across environment, social, and governance. The other emerging trend is the rise of new and expansive stakeholder groups who want to see this information. The last is the proliferation of platforms and channels across owned, earned, and paid that can be used to tell the sustainability story and include data that go well beyond a single annual report.

The individuals I spoke with had some good insight into what they wanted to see from reports and the proliferation of ESG data going forward.

Procurement

For the business-to-business company, customer and prospect procurement departments will usually ask about a report. Is it published annually? It's generally a check-the-box exercise and does not go any further, other than as an attachment to the submission, unless that commercial customer has ambitious sustainability goals themselves. That's when someone from the internal ESG team will comb through the report, looking for ways to collaborate and expand a commercial engagement into an enterprise solution. It could be around emission reductions and will usually come from their sustainability organization, not the procurement side.

Investors and Fund Managers

Current investing is driven by an incomprehensible amount of analytics all around the minute financial aspects of a company. What investors expect to be coming is a way to do that for ESG. We will see, over the next five to ten years, an explosion of platforms and products that collect, synthesize, and harmonize all the environmental and sustainability data. This will include a look at data and intention or vision. So that, when you get market volatility, you can show which strategies hold up. That should give comfort to investors that sustainability vision and the cascading environment, social and governance programs and resource allocation are integrated for the long term.

The big question I had for this group was how important the storytelling or brand alignment part of sustainability narratives mattered when assessing for inclusion in ESG funds or analyzing within certain fund classes. For this group, they wanted to see alignment at the executive level. Everyone on the investor call or in the C-suite should be able to repeat the company mission statement and vision, and how this aligns with the ESG vision. There is a strong expectation that sustainability really lives at that level. There cannot be any inconsistency between what brands tell investors and consumers. Companies need a sustainability vision. The report shows how companies comply with the rules so there is no chance to be criticized for bad data.

Fund managers look at ESG reports and data primarily for a risk assessment—they are looking for the negative effects from bad news, or a slowed positive effect for good news. Investors are looking for ESG data that can identify monetization moments. It's all about data, not storytelling. According to the investors I spoke with, no one is making money off ESG because most fund managers are still looking for short-term versus long-term payoff. When investors participate in ESG, it is because they believe in it. High net worth investors are told that they will take a hit and will not see any short-term gain. ESG is still a long bet for value, but a good risk indicator for the short term.

Nonprofits and Activists

According to those in nonprofits who review reports to assess how companies are meeting commitments or living up to purpose promises, annual sustainability reports should be shortened and streamlined. This stakeholder group wants brands to provide data in a common framework (like the Global Reporting Initiative or Task Force on Climate-related Financial Disclosures) and include an overarching vision, strategies to get there and the robust and assured data that allows for year-over-year comparisons. According to the person I spoke with, there are too many stories, too many pretty pictures and anecdotes. They do not want or need all the marketing content and any "glitzy" content. What they are looking for is context, such as strategy for the progress being reported, and proof that the company vision is long-term and committed to achieving the targets that are specific and timebound.

Consumers and Employees

These stakeholders consistently look for updated information about how a company is living up to its purpose and meeting commitments to DEI progress or climate change. As we have shown, research over and over verifies that consumers, and most importantly Gen Z, have a sophisticated understanding of climate change issues and the complexity of societal equity. They are not expecting perfection, but they do demand progress. Employee attitudes mirror consumers. In fact, these two are really the same cohort. If anything, data shows that Gen Z workers hold their employers to a higher say/do standard than brands they buy from. If there is no alignment of values, these employees will look for another job.

The value for a company in writing these reports is in making sure they are in line with what the business is already doing, and essentially making low-hanging fruit more valuable than it otherwise would be because maybe no one knows about it, or no one knows how impactful it is. Brands must control the outbound sustainability narrative to make sure the story does not get told incorrectly, to ensure that the complexity is explained, that the context is set. Then, the data serves as evidence about how the story connects, and programs support objectives.

ESG Data

Rating and ranking indices are constantly scraping data for algorithm assessments of a company's performance against climate commitments, emissions, waste, water, diversity in leadership, supply chain risk, etc. An ESG/sustainability communications program needs to be comprehensive, transparent, and rooted in data that is provided on a regular and findable basis and include the aspirational and anecdotal stories that bring it to life.

ESG data is showing up in more places because better tools exist to hold businesses accountable for both their financial performance and their commitment to ESG. An individual or institutional investor can easily evaluate different investment funds around return on investment and ESG with tools such as the publicly available MSCI ESG Research ETF Overview, the Socially Responsible ETF database, or the Morningstar Sustainability Rating. When you layer on data that is available through private mechanisms such as 401(k)s or other fund analyses, the result is an empowered and informed stakeholder.

ESG activities, metrics and reporting are beginning to become integrated into many organizations' information management systems. Mainstreaming ESG norms into regular operations is the real objective of ESG programming. The reporting aspect of ESG will become more standardized, but the choice of policies and practices upon which an organization's ESG platform is built will continue to be a differentiator in stakeholders' minds and influence their affinity toward the organization's products and services.

Data-driven systems will become the backbone of good ESG programming and reporting. There is a significant increase in demand for hard data to track and report the wide range of issues included under the broad umbrella of ESG. Effective metrics and industry standards are essential tools to provide the data demanded.

Owned, Earned, and Paid Platforms

It's important to provide a big picture vision of what companies want to achieve supported by measurable goals and objectives. This is the same formula companies use to set performance goals against their long-term vision—typical corporate communications content. The new opportunity is to connect the dots and integrate sustainability with high-level business strategy. And tell the story over and over, with a constant cadence, to the widest range of stakeholders. Investors, employees, customers, partners, community leaders, NGOs, and activists are all paying attention not just to the stories but also to the details within ESG/sustainability performance.

Companies need a robust communications strategy, program, campaigns, and tentpole moments to ensure data, stories, anecdotes, and inspirational and reactive content are produced and disseminated constantly and consistently across owned, earned, and paid channels. Messaging, spokesperson training, press releases, social posts, paid media, partner comms, internal campaigns, and investor communications are all part of a best-in-class program.

A brand's sustainability narrative and ongoing communications about the vision and progress help define the company's character. How a company lives out its values will be clear by the choices it makes, the problems it solves, and what it doesn't do in the face of challenges. When there's a say/do gap between the purpose promise and the brand experience, there's a problem. A company will begin to experience impact—social media chatter, negative media stories, decline in revenue, perhaps even dips in share price—until the say/do gap is addressed on both sides of that equation.

Integration with Marketing

An area where sustainability and purpose messaging is finding its way is with marketing—on the website, in advertising content and on product or packaging, and in store and online retail experiences. In fact, these owned assets are some of the best channels where brands can control the narrative and use the "real estate" to continuously update and educate consumers about the intricacies of the environmental and social dimensions of both the product and the company.

One of the most authentic ways to market the sustainability narrative is to tell how the product was made, where it was made, what ingredients it was made with, who made it, and what to do with it after it's done. The fullness of that story should be comprehensive and transparent, a brand's first defense against greenwashing. In fact, allowing just some small progress program or single product attribute to be the carrier of sustainability communications is a type of greenwashing.

The apparel sector has made some strides in comprehensive product innovation. For example, Everlane launched its ReNew and ReKnit fabric, made from plastic bottles, to be used in clothing and accessories. In this case, the products and what they are made with is itself the story worth telling because it moves beyond sustaining the status quo into solving environmental issues through product design. Messaging about the effort is part of their sustainability report, is included on the initiative's web page as part of the product descriptions, and was announced in 2018 as a major plastics initiative (Everlane, 2022).

Measuring Success

Sustainability and ESG communications success can be measured as all communications are measured—who did we reach? What do they know about our performance? How do they feel about us as a company and about our products? Have we built trust so that, when we run into challenges, they will be patient with us as we work to course-correct? Answers to these questions can be gained through surveys, online questionnaires, call center intake, media coverage tracking, social media listening, and other metrics used to track overall brand sentiment and audience attitudes. Adding measurement for the sustainability narrative uptake is becoming a best practice.

Expert Opinion: From Sacrificial to Irresistible by Annie Longsworth

In 2008 I had the great fortune to meet Annie Longsworth at the first Sustainable Brands conference in New Orleans. Over bowls of gumbo we discovered we shared a perspective that compelling communications and meeting consumers where they are critical to the culture shift needed for a thriving planet. We have been collaborators and friends ever since.

The following is her perspective on the trajectory of sustainability.

Fifteen years ago, the selection of "sustainable" products available to consumers was essentially limited to the bottom shelf of the toothpaste aisle or self-serve bins at a grocery co-op. While I applaud those pioneers, it's not a big surprise that their products didn't have mass appeal. They were directed to a minority—tree-huggers, health nuts, and naturalists. For years brands have been asking consumers to sacrifice for the sake of the planet. Wear clothes that are scratchy and stiff and only come in earth tones. Use a deodorant or a toilet bowl cleaner that may or may not be effective. Purchase foods that aren't conveniently packaged for a commute. Build your house with materials that cost twice as much. Buy a car that won't go as far as you want to go. All of these "benefits" were touted on behalf of saving a planet that most people only recently started to appreciate is in need of saving.

Two key elements of this equation have changed, slowly but surely, and they are as co-dependent as you can get. One, brands slowly started producing sustainable products that still appealed on the most basic purchase decision points—efficacy and quality. (Price parity is still yet to come.) And two, consumers started demanding options that were less dependent on non-renewable resources and produced with less energy intensive systems. These shifts happened in parallel, but in fits and starts. Why would McDonald's risk a change to its beef supply if consumers would reject it? Why would consumers ask for a "greener" Big Mac if they didn't know it was an option or even a problem?

Over the years, survey after survey reported that consumers wanted to choose more sustainable products, and yet their actions belie their conviction. The result was to blame the fickle consumer, but the real problem was consumers didn't have viable choices that didn't require them to sacrifice what they saw as basic requirements—comfort, flavor, convenience. "Eco-friendly" was a cherry, but not the sundae.

Another movement was happening at the same time: communication. Again, this was being addressed in two fundamental ways, one in the science community and one through marketing. When I launched Cohn & Wolfe's global sustainability practice in 2007, communication was not considered critical to a sustainability strategy. The thinking then (by the few leading-edge companies that recognized the opportunity of climate change) was to just do the work and not worry about telling the exciting stories of innovation and impact. Many companies missed their competitive opportunity to build consumer loyalty (not to mention slow the speed of global warming) because they were either too scared to be first and not good enough, or because they were humble to the point of irrelevance.

The science community didn't know how to talk about our increasingly dire climate crisis without sounding too, well, scientific, or political. Those who were trying to wave a red flag came across as fringe and Chicken Little-ish, which did little to persuade a population that, in 2008–09, was just trying to put food on the table. Similarly, as brands slowly started testing language and behavior that might appeal to a greener audience, they were either too vague or too bold in their claims, which hurt credibility either way. No one wanted to give up precious real estate on their packaging or advertising to tout an environmental benefit that was unlikely to sway a buyer.

From a marketing perspective, the big shift I experienced and helped herald was to move from sacrifice to irresistible, which, of course, was only possible if the products and services were truly desired by consumers. One of the strategies was to reorder the benefits of a sustainable solution. A classic example is the Toyota Prius, which initially launched as a hybrid car that would save the planet. Eventually Prius recognized the main benefit to its consumer was the significant financial savings realized through less fuel, which, by the way, also helped the planet. With this shift in how it communicated to prospective buyers, Prius gained market share and suddenly everyone wanted one. Another example is the launch of Method, which had an ambition to be aesthetically pleasing enough to be left next to the sink rather than stored under it. With its tear drop bottles and bright colors, Method modernized dish soap without screaming about its chemical-free solution or reduced-plastic packaging.

This is not to say that environmental and social benefits should be hidden, especially as younger consumers demand more from brands and are putting their dollars behind their beliefs. It's meant to point out the evolution of sustainability communication. Farm-to-table says fresh and healthful in a way that pesticide-free does not. Value chain says fair in a way that supply chain does not. And free-range says humane in a way that cage-free does not.

Sustainability is not about scratchy clothes and fear. It's about abundance and joy, innovation, and opportunity. The language we use must be honest, yes, and it must be inspiring. It requires an ongoing collaboration among brands, consumers, scientists, government, and marketers to continue to shift from sacrificial to irresistible.

References

Everlane (2022) Our environmental initiatives, Everlane, www.everlane.com/sustainability (archived at https://perma.cc/SNU4-PUL7)

Governance & Accountability Institute (2021) 92% of S&P 500® companies and 70% of Russell 1000® companies published sustainability reports in 2020, G&A Institute research shows, Governance & Accountability Institute, www.globenewswire.com/news-release/2021/11/16/2335435/0/en/92-of-S-P-500-Companies-and-70-of-Russell-1000-Companies-Published-Sustainability-Reports-in-2020-G-A-Institute-Research-Shows.html (archived at https://perma.cc/Q7C9-8W42)

Greenhouse Gas Protocol (2022) FAQ, Greenhouse Gas Protocol, https://ghgprotocol.org/sites/default/files/standards_supporting/FAQ.pdf (archived at https://perma.cc/QNY6-N23T)

SB Brands for Good (2021) New research from Sustainable Brands and Ipsos highlights consumers' willingness to leverage their buying power to support companies' good work, SB Brands for Good, https://sbbrandsforgood.com/2021-11/new-research-from-sustainable-brands-and-ipsos-highlights-consumers-willingness-to-leverage-their-buying-power-to-support-companies-good-work (archived at https://perma.cc/HPQ7-KYAX)

Engaging Stakeholders and Collaborators

09

Progress Requires a System of Change Agents

There is a growing realization among my peers and colleagues in the purpose and sustainability sector, especially those who have been doing this work since the early 2000s, that we can no longer effect change in isolation. We all need to be working collectively, in a systems approach, linking the efforts of competitors, supply chains, consumers, and the public sector in addressing climate change and social inequality.

In the early days of this sustainability wave, which I described in Chapter 1 as the "fourth wave," we were all working at the individual company level to drive mostly internal change. We helped form green teams and sought ways to reduce paper use, eliminate Styrofoam in cafeterias, deploy rooftop solar, and a myriad of other organizational changes. We referred to this as "low hanging fruit" and it got lots of attention as examples of corporate social responsibility. But we are in new territory now. Once the easy wins had been achieved, it became clear that to substantially reduce harmful impact or create net positive solutions that restore habitats and eliminate entrenched barriers to equity, it will take a collective effort.

Companies with a sustainability strategy, even if newly formed, will have conducted a materiality assessment which includes input from a range of stakeholders as to the most material environmental, social and governance challenges the business faces within the context of business strategy. Such a process requires the creation of a stakeholder map that includes both internal and external groups upon whom the company depends in meeting its business objectives. These typically include employees, customers, investors, NGOs, regulators, and suppliers.

Stakeholder management is a classic business strategy, one that begins with identifying all those groups involved in any business function or process, auditing their attitudes and requirements, and then deploying an ongoing mechanism for consistently engaging or pulsing for feedback. This is certainly true for sustainability strategy and ESG program implementation. What makes this exercise a bit tricky is how interdependent, and in some cases at odds, these stakeholders can be among each other. And, given the urgent need to make progress on climate change as well as the socially disruptive aspects of extreme weather, often companies need active participation by a range of stakeholders to have a chance at meeting goals. And making real progress at improving ecosystems and lives.

We will take a look at each of the standard stakeholders as identified in a materiality assessment, and how to ensure active engagement and collect ongoing feedback. This stakeholder group is a good place to start when identifying participants needed for accelerating overall environmental progress and driving more equitable impact. However, sometimes, a broader set of specific stakeholders is warranted in order to assemble all of the players needed to drive change, most notably for those companies looking to accelerate progress on a specific or material issue.

For example, companies trying to lower greenhouse gas emissions may be converting gasoline fleet vehicles into electric vehicles. I have seen companies who are making that move as an internal program also look at participating in coalitions that include automotive companies, local governments, regional utility companies, and software companies who are all involved in building out the charging, storage, and tracking infrastructure. It will take all of these companies, often in a formal coalition like the Corporate Electric Vehicle Alliance, to speed deployment of EV fleets (Ceres, 2022).

Starting at the System Level

I am a corporate board director for Sustainable Brands and have spent almost a decade also serving on its Advisory Board. This global professional organization has led the definition and transformation of brands into sustainable brands through a range of tools, content, conferences, and working groups. As described in Chapter 3, the SB Brand Transformation Roadmap guides companies on the journey from conventional business to sustainable brand, and includes a self-assessment tool that enables any company to see where they stand today and then chart their course forward. It was deliberately built with a systems approach and helps companies look across stakeholders to see how engagement and collaboration will accelerate progress not only within the organization but also out into driving culture change as well (Hagen, 2018).

Broadly speaking, systems thinking is a broad term to describe a way of making sense of the complexity of the world by looking at it in terms of wholes and relationships rather than by splitting it down into its parts. It incorporates awareness of the circular nature of the world and an awareness of the role that structure can play in creating conditions. It also allows for a recognition that there are governing systems operating that we might be unaware of and creates space to explore both designed and unintended consequences inherent in any system or series of actions and choices.

This is a perfect framework for exploring engaging stakeholders and deploying collaborators in driving positive outcomes. Regardless of the issue or challenge—from reducing greenhouse gas emissions to eliminating plastic waste, from ensuring pay equity to preventing racial bias in decision-making—analyzing each issue as part of a bigger system than simply in isolation creates a mechanism for collective progress. In social change and the nonprofit world, this is known as a theory of change and its exploration of the interrelation between organizational outputs (like medicines or access) to impacts (such as the number of people reached or signed up) and the tangible outcomes in people's lives (such as better health or more financial assets).

There are a few key components for exploration that give teams a way to assess an issue and assemble the necessary players to come together. When mapping stakeholders in a systems change exercise, it is important to begin by zooming way out and looking as expansively as possible at the interconnected relationships between all of the players to determine who, besides the individual company, needs to be in the room to solve the problem. Many times, this will reveal a cast of unlikely partners who, if they can find common ground, can work together to address a shared issue, or at least reduce friction in the system that might be preventing progress.

Brands see revenues grow when they build products and services to address social challenges or authentically address new audiences whose marginalized status may have made them invisible before. They see costs falling when they increase employee engagement and use resources more efficiently. Their organizations thrive in environments which foster compassion, loyalty, and trust. All of these serve as motivation for engaging a range of stakeholders in problem identification and solutions development.

Figure 9.1   Sustainability stakeholders, 2022

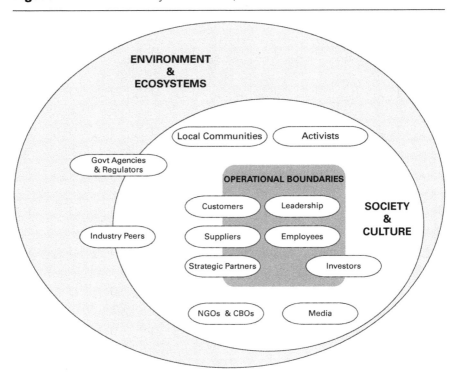

Prioritizing Employees

Many leadership teams have yet to fully commit to engaging with and learning from the people they are trying to help and influence. This is especially true when it comes to employees and a diverse customer set. Often executives think they know how employees feel about a certain topic or issue, but it's important to question how they believe they know this. Most employee surveys or even regular ERG focus groups are not asking about attitudes regarding social issues or environmental concerns. They tend to measure loyalty, engagement, and overall job satisfaction—which are extremely important to consistently measure. In addition, I recommend also creating methods for pulsing employee attitudes about the company's response to current events, rising issues or long-term challenges like climate change. These exercises will likely reveal what a recent CNBC Momentive workplace happiness survey found. Thirty-two percent of workers say they support their companies' speaking out on social issues, regardless of whether they agree with them (Ewell, 2022).

Employees are one of the most critical pressure points on executives who are considering how to wade into social issues and how to navigate the choppy waters of social media reactions. Executives watch social media chatter from individuals and political groups (often amplified by bot activity) attack "woke" corporations for taking positions on issues such as racism, gender expression, bodily autonomy, or access to voting. These same executives are also getting employee pressure to show up, voice support, and change policies relating to cultural and social issues.

Management has two alternatives in meeting employee expectations that seem to run counter to other external voices. The first is essentially defensive and prioritizes what general counsel advises as the least risky in response to what executives experience as conflicting stakeholder expectations. Companies that operate this way will distill justice, equity, diversity, inclusion (JEDI) into essentially a diversity activity and prioritize counting and reporting on various employee groups rather than the alternative—a more expansive view of what the underlying systems are and how they can contribute to inequality or different experiences by different employee groups.

An alternative response to pressure is a type of employee engagement that requires humility and leaders willing to acknowledge that they have blind spots and do not have all the answers. These executives, many of whom I have worked with, are willing to admit that their perspective is limited, their lived experience different, so they will seek out other viewpoints. In the era of quiet quitting and a post-pandemic Great Resignation, leaders who adopt a humanistic approach to meeting employee expectations will find more success in assuring a stable and engaged workforce.

Employee activism and unionization are on the rise globally as employees use their voices and collective influence to react to political and societal tensions. This has caught most companies off guard. Whether asking their employers to publicly aligning with Black Lives Matter and the #MeToo movement, and acknowledge the climate change crisis, employees are making their views known and looking to their employers for an explicit corporate position, especially as these brands promote their purpose and ESG goals.

Employees are unionizing and organizing about more than just pay, discrimination, and working conditions, although those remain top issues. They are also organizing and taking action around the kind of work they are being asked to do. This is especially true with technology companies. At Meta (formerly Facebook) and Alphabet (formerly Google), engineers and other employees have walked out and organized protests to voice their concern about company projects or products that have proven to be problematic in society or contribute to environmental harm. For example, in 2018 Google employees opposed business decisions and product development projects that they deemed unethical, such as developing artificial intelligence for the US Defense Department and providing technology to US Customs and Border Protection (Conger, 2021).

Within the advertising and communications industry, there has been a well-established practice among some agencies who have a stated policy that prohibits them from working on campaigns benefiting tobacco or firearm companies. In addition to a specific policy on the types of accounts agencies will or won't work with, there can also be a management practice that allows team members to opt out of accounts that the individual may have a strong personal opinion about. For the first time, I am seeing some agency colleagues extend their list of bad actors with whom they will not work to fossil fuel companies or projects with clients that restrict access to reproductive healthcare. While there have been no official employee protests or organizing efforts, a quiet change is underway internally within many agencies.

Engaging the Supply Chain

The supply chain is a critical part of achieving sustainability goals, across environmental, social, and governance aspects. Much of a company's Scope 3 emissions will come from the supply chain.

As we have already reviewed, the GHG Protocol defines Scope 3 emissions as all of the indirect emissions that occur in the value chain of the reporting company, including both upstream into the supply chain and downstream through distribution and transportation of products to customer use. It is easy to see how difficult it is not only to measure the environmental and social aspects of each of these links in the value chain, but also to effect change. If an electronics company contracts with a contract manufacturer for electronic parts, most of the time they are just one of several brands contracting for similar parts. The contract manufacturer has little incentive to meet carbon goals, use renewable energy, or ensure safe working conditions that go beyond local regulations—if any exist at all. Even as brands make Scope 3 commitments and are striving to engage with suppliers and create low-carbon and easily recyclable products and services to reduce value chains emissions, it is hard to do with little to no leverage.

Increasing awareness about Scope 3 emissions is being carefully watched by groups like the Science Based Targets initiative. In fact, if supply chain GHG represents more than 40 percent of a company's overall emissions, the Science Based Targets initiative requires that a target is put in place to cover the impact (Labutong, 2018; CDP et al, 2021) Which means those companies need to be working with suppliers to reduce their carbon footprint. This is why more and more B2B companies are developing supplier programs aimed at adding requirements for suppliers to have their own net-zero targets, make public commitments around renewable energy use, and participate in questionnaires that document answers to questions about worker safety, progress against goals, and adherence to regulatory requirements regarding labor and pay. These questionnaires are then supplemented with annual spot factory audits with certification of conditions a prerequisite for ongoing contracts. These are not perfect systems and there are many cases where suppliers create one set of conditions for the auditor and then revert back to less-than-ideal conditions once the officials have left the factory floor. But short of constant surveillance, self-reporting and spot audits are the tools available.

Online global fashion retail platform Zalando has built on its commitment to carbon neutrality across its own operations by committing to having 90 percent of its key suppliers set their own science-based targets by 2025 (Zalando, 2022). Zalando has also signed up to the Sustainable Apparel Coalition to use a new module that will make sustainability assessments mandatory for its private labels and partner brands, like Nike, Burlington, and others, sold on its platform (2021).

Convincing Investors

According to 2021 joint research from the World Economic Forum and Accenture, when executive teams deploy strong positive alignment across multiple stakeholders to improve sustainability performance, they financially outperform those where alignment is weakest by 13 percent (World Economic Forum, 2022). Over and over, the connection between sustainability and financial performance is strengthening and demonstrable, as the WEF/Accenture research shows (Accenture, 2021).

During the last two decades, I have seen the dialogue in boardrooms change. Early on, companies were able to avoid speaking on current issues, like climate change, social inequality, or fair working conditions. Today, opting out of those discussions either in the board-room or even publicly is far from optional. Publicly traded organizations must discuss and invest in sustainability and environmental, social, and corporate governance or risk incurring significant economic costs.

Because investment in ESG has accelerated dramatically, due in part to the pandemic, extreme weather caused by global warming, and social unrest, more than $51.1 billion was poured into sustainable funds in 2020, compared with less than $5 billion in 2015 (Versace and Abssy, 2022). It is becoming widely accepted that companies with strong ESG programs are more likely to boost shareholder returns, improve long-term viability, and build a positive reputation with consumers, stakeholders, and employees.

Engaging the investor stakeholder means providing evidence that sustainability is a strategy, clear governance ensures continuity of progress as well as informed decision-making, and executives are being incentivized to meet ESG goals alongside financial. The trick for communicators is helping investors see both ESG's near-term effects as well as the long-term gains and be willing to apply patient capital so that companies can deploy ESG solutions.

To sort through the noise, a nonprofit called As You Sow runs a free database called FossilFreeFunds.org that ranks all funds on Wall Street by environmental measures. They led pay proposals aimed at GM and Valero and hold the position that ESG linkage should be tied to long-term bonuses, rather than annual payouts, thereby incentivizing the type of long-term thinking that many ESG tradeoffs require.

The use of ESG factors in determining executive pay has not been extensively tracked or well defined but that is changing. According to a report from consultancy Semler Brossy (2022), 70 percent of S&P 500 companies incorporated some type of ESG factor into executive bonus plans in 2022, up from 57 percent the year prior. Tying pay to diversity and inclusion goals, or a carbon footprint, were the two factors that saw the largest year-on-year increases, the firm said.

Xylem, a water conservation company, is a rare example of a company that has baked social goals into annual and long-term bonuses. In 2021, it offered special performance stock bonuses on ESG goals. These shares comprise up to 15 per cent of total pay for all executives at the company (Xylem, 2022). This is an example of the growing application of a DEI lens as evidenced in the 2021 completed proxy season according to Russell Reynolds Associates, a leadership advice and recruiting consultancy. The "S" of ESG is now getting the investor attention it deserves.

Working With Activists

A question I often get from brands is whether or how to engage with the most vocal and inquisitive activist groups who are constantly asking companies to fill out questionnaires, provide detailed information about policies and programs, and threaten to lower a ranking or call out what these activists see as bad performance. In one instance, I was working with a retailer that was being assessed by As You Sow for DEI progress. Their sustainability team received a very specific set of questions about religious freedoms and expression allowances in their stores. What I recommended was to cite existing policies and sections from the employee handbook which provided good guidance to employees on what was appropriate to wear and how to get time off for specific observances. As You Sow is the investor accountability activist group described earlier in relation to climate policy. They are also looking for company progress on DEI commitments as well.

This is a great example, because most companies should have these policies in place. At the most basic level, religion is protected in the United States by the Equal Employment Opportunity Commission (2022). It is illegal for employers to discriminate against someone (applicant or employee) on the basis of race, color, religion, sex (including gender identity, sexual orientation, and pregnancy), national origin, age (40 or older), disability or genetic information; and an employer is required to reasonably accommodate an employee's religious beliefs or practices, unless doing so would cause difficulty or expense for the employer. This means an employer may have to make reasonable adjustments at work that will allow the employee to practice his or her religion, such as allowing an employee to voluntarily swap shifts with a co-worker so that he or she can attend religious services.

There is another activist group that is tracking religious issues specifically. The Religious Freedom and Business Foundation (RFBF) established a benchmark for the state of corporate America's inclusion of religion in DEI initiatives in 2020. Its Religious Equity, Diversity, and Inclusion Index identified the top 10 companies committed to inclusive, faith-friendly workplaces (Religious Freedom and Business Foundation, 2022).

There are a number of accommodations that companies can deploy to satisfy the questions or rankings of organizations like RFBF that, when communicated, can help prevent negative pushback or lowered rankings as well. For example, when it comes to religious minority policies in the workplace, some suggested ideas that can meet activist requests could include:

- Dress/attire standards: Ensure that "dress for your day" policies expressly communicate openness for employees to dress consistently with their religious imperatives (including head-coverings, facial hair and modest clothing).

- Religious holidays: Maintain transparency across the company regarding religious holiday leave, including clear direction to managers to ensure consistency across business lines. Best-in-class companies offer three to five floating holidays annually.

- Food/meals: Companies should offer kosher and halal-certified meal options, or at a minimum offer vegetarian options, at company cafeterias. Provide options for those with religious dietary needs when ordering food for meetings or events.

- Prayer/meditation space: Dedicate space at company headquarters and across all facilities for employees who desire to pray, meditate, or otherwise seek reflection during the workday.

- Faith-based employee resource groups: Encourage and facilitate the creation of faith-based (including interfaith) ERGs which can establish mentoring programs, provide educational programs, connect employees with role models, and inform the company about upcoming holidays.

- Religious non-discrimination accountability: Establish and publicize the steps the company will take to respond to internal allegations of religious discrimination and integrate religious coexistence and anti-hate education within unconscious bias training.

- Religious coexistence in company's social footprint: Develop procedures to address potential religious intolerance or bigotry in the corporation's products and services (for example, if a corporation offers a product for sale that is bigoted toward religious minorities, including hate imagery).

That's a detailed look at just one often overlooked DEI dimension. Like other identities including race, ethnicity, gender or orientation, a company can create a robust set of policies and practices similar to those described for accommodating a variety of faith expressions. You can also apply this type of transparency about climate or other environmental challenges coming from activist groups. The recommended approach is one of openness, transparency, humility, and willingness to learn more. It can also include a two-way dialogue so that brands have a chance to teach activist groups more about the challenges faced by companies looking to address issues across complexities.

Many communicators are wary about speaking out on issues unless the issue is directly related to the company's business operations or customer base. Experience in dealing with activists is limited since most companies have an informal "hands off, no comment" response. I think this is short sighted. While there are risks in talking directly with those groups challenging a company over its policies and progress, there are benefits to bringing them closer in.

An activist group within the communications and advertising industry, Clean Creatives, is starting to step up its actions in calling out agencies whose creative concepts and campaigns have been used by fossil fuel companies to obfuscate or greenwash the effects that fossil fuels have on the environment over the last several decades. These activists, along with the agency employees who are quietly declining these projects mentioned earlier, are having an effect on the realities that both agency leaders and client brands must take into account when navigating change management.

Including Politicians, Campaigns and Trade Associations

Corporate political responsibility (CPR) is emerging as a new dimension in sustainability consideration and offers a novel look at how brands are being scrutinized for involvement with political stakeholders. Typically, a company's public affairs and government relations functions manage the decisions made to support candidates, lobbying efforts, political action committees. These departments also set corporate policy around how a company will either support or oppose legislation and if membership in trade associations that have robust lobbying initiatives is in alignment with the company's best interests. Often, these activities are done in isolation from sustainability strategies and can even be in opposition to publicly stated environmental or social commitments.

Additionally, a 2021 Integral/Harris Poll study (Integral, 2021) found that 48 percent of US respondents said they should be able to express themselves politically at work, with 51 percent of respondents saying they are comfortable doing so, especially true with Millennials (McCarty, 2021). The younger and soon to be largest worker age groups do not distinguish between work and life when it comes to being visible and active on social media. Voicing their political opinions is simply part of that reality.

The emergence of CPR is, in my mind, the last and latest bastion of the say/do gap. Brands will need to take a close look at the congruence between their environment and social commitments and the splashy marketing campaigns they develop to communicate progress, and the often-hidden political actions taken on their behalf by political action committees or trade associations.

Companies struggle for congruence between their brand and normal operations. Alignment is even harder on more complex issues such as sustainability, inequality, social justice, and education. Many times, the CSO, brand management, DEI, and government affairs all come with very different assumptions, priorities, and strategies. Without a proactive, principled way to reconcile these views, companies' words and actions diverge. Consistency is one of the most basic ways people know if they can trust a brand to do what it says it is going to do. Simple inconsistency between words and action will be seen as intentional greenwashing or hypocrisy—terrible outcomes for both reputation and impact.

References

Accenture (2021) *Shaping the Sustainable Organization: How responsible leaders create lasting value and equitable impact for all stakeholders*, Accenture, www.accenture.com/_acnmedia/Thought-Leadership-Assets/PDF-5/Accenture-Shaping-the-Sustainable-Organization-Report.pdf (archived at https://perma.cc/9VF2-DBEF)

CDP et al (2021) *SBTi Corporate Net-Zero Standard*, United Nations Global Compact, World Resources Institute and World Wide Fund for Nature, https://sciencebasedtargets.org/resources/files/Net-Zero-Standard.pdf (archived at https://perma.cc/A8CC-FJP3)

Ceres (2022) Major fleet owners urge smart, rapid build-out of electric vehicle infrastructure, Ceres, https://ceres.org/news-center/press-releases/major-fleet-owners-urge-smart-rapid-build-out-electric-vehicle (archived at https://perma.cc/4MJN-GBQJ)

Conger, K (2021) Hundreds of Google employees unionize, culminating years of activism, *New York Times*, www.nytimes.com/2021/01/04/technology/google-employees-union.html (archived at https://perma.cc/AZ6E-VSGJ)

Equal Employment Opportunity Commission (2022) What you should know about the EEOC and religious discrimination, Equal Employment Opportunity Commission, www.eeoc.gov/wysk/what-you-should-know-about-eeoc-and-religious-discrimination (archived at https://perma.cc/JA2Z-5P8A)

Ewell, K (2022) CNBC Momentive workforce happiness index: May 2022, Momentive, www.momentive.ai/en/blog/cnbc-workforce-survey-may-2022 (archived at https://perma.cc/ED37-NXAF)

Greenhouse Gas Protocol (2022) FAQ, Greenhouse Gas Protocol, https://ghgprotocol.org/sites/default/files/standards_supporting/FAQ.pdf (archived at https://perma.cc/U7XY-SPET)

Hagen, K (2018) Redesigning for success in sustainability: Introducing the SB brand transformation roadmap, Sustainable Brands, https://sustainablebrands.com/library/view/sb-18-vancouver-keynote-redesigning-for-success-in-sustainability-introducing-the-sb-brand-transformation-roadmap (archived at https://perma.cc/PCT7-4SFQ)

Integral (2021) *Integral Employee Activation Index: Employee readiness to support organizational goals*, Integral, www.teamintegral.com/wp-content/uploads/2022/06/Integral-Employee-Activation-Index-2021.pdf (archived at https://perma.cc/7FLX-NN3P)

Labutong, N (2018) How can companies address their Scope 3 greenhouse gas emissions? Science Based Targets, https://sciencebasedtargets.org/blog/how-can-companies-address-their-scope-3-greenhouse-gas-emissions (archived at https://perma.cc/YUC2-TG2F)

McCarty, E (2021) Integral and the Harris Poll find employees are giving employers a performance review, Integral, www.teamintegral.com/2021/employee-activation-index/ (archived at https://perma.cc/CZ4F-U69G)

Religious Freedom and Business Foundation (2022) Corporate religious equity, diversity and inclusion (REDI) index, Religious Freedom and Business Foundation, https://religiousfreedomandbusiness.org/redi (archived at https://perma.cc/LWX9-24YT)

Semler Brossy (2022) *ESG + Incentives 2022 Report*, Semler Brossy, https://semlerbrossy.com/wp-content/uploads/2022/07/ESG-Report-Issue-1-2022.pdf (archived at https://perma.cc/W9AU-844D)

Temple-West, P (2022) ESG activists see executive pay as tool for raising standards, *Financial Times*, www.ft.com/content/36e3143b-6c6f-4991-b310-46c07e7c3e02 (archived at https://perma.cc/3HQQ-KAKN)

Versace, C and Abssy, M (2022) How Millennials and Gen Z are driving growth behind ESG, www.nasdaq.com/articles/how-millennials-and-gen-z-are-driving-growth-behind-esg (archived at https://perma.cc/458Q-A242)

World Economic Forum (2022) How stakeholder alignment on sustainability unlocks a competitive advantage, WEF, www.weforum.org/agenda/2022/02/how-to-strengthen-sustainability-by-engaging-with-stakeholders (archived at https://perma.cc/QW77-58FX)

Xylem (2022) *2022 Proxy Statement: Notice of annual meeting of shareholders*, Xylem, www.xylem.com/siteassets/investors/proxy-statement-final-print-ready.pdf (archived at https://perma.cc/FAC5-VM88)

Zalando (2021) *Sustainable Sourcing Policy*, Zalando, https://corporate.zalando.com/sites/default/files/media-download/Zalando_SE_Sustainable_Sourcing_Policy.pdf (archived at https://perma.cc/3JL3-SFVR)

Zalando (2022), Reducing our carbon footprint, Zalando, https://corporate.zalando.com/en/our-impact/reducing-our-carbon-footprint (archived at https://perma.cc/TE52-EQLW)

Communications 10 For Good

The New Language of Business Includes Purpose and Sustainability

Communication is an integral part of articulating and operationalizing a purposeful brand. In fact, it is the key reason I rejoined Porter Novelli in 2019 after a 15-year hiatus. During those 15 years, I honed my sustainability skills, becoming a practitioner and strategist as well as a behavior change communicator.

During my years at a progressive communications firm, I worked with foundations, NGOs, and activists as clients who were trying to create a positive impact through communications based on theories of change. During this three-year stint, I became acquainted with the concept that social change is possible when key messages are developed based upon deep ethnographic, somatic, psychographic, and immersive in-depth interview research. I had spent my career prior to this stint in progressive activism studying the attributes and motivations of consumers. I knew how to segment consumer groups by race, region, income, education level and how to persuade people to buy something.

But this new work brought me face to face with the reality that we are all citizens—not just consumers of products. I learned to segment and understand groups of people based on beliefs, values, and group affiliation. And then I began to understand how those layered identities affected how people saw the world, how they voted (or didn't), what actions they were willing to participate in, and how they might be persuaded to care for themselves or others in new ways.

Two faith-based projects that have stayed with me were the exploration of mainstream US Christians and their attitudes and beliefs around marriage equality, and climate change. I am not a religious person, despite having been raised traditionally Catholic (maybe because of it). But as the product of Jesuit education, I can understand and have an appreciation for the structures of religious groups and doctrine. I certainly have a spiritual dimension that makes space for many religious rites and the personal relationship many people have with their church communities as well as their interior faith life. This proved to be a good basis from which to work on projects that aimed to understand the mindsets, biases, and potential readiness to hear and engage with both acceptance of LGBTQ+ marriage and what at the time were seen as highly politicized terms, global warming and climate change.

In both cases, taking the time to deeply understand the doctrinal teachings inside various religious sects as it was applied to either same gender marriage or stewardship of God's creation—the planet—we developed campaigns that made real change possible. Those years gave me the chance to see not only how to interrogate assumptions and stereotypes but also apply communications and storytelling in support of societal change rather than market expansion.

I spent another few years at a British Standards Institution environment, health and safety consulting group, working alongside ergonomists, industrial hygienists, and environmental scientists to deliver technical and legally compliant safety programs or air/water/waste programs that addressed the operational aspects of manufacturing and transportation. This phase of my career gave me the opportunity to work alongside highly trained and experienced worker safety experts who audited factories and research labs, looking for falling and tripping hazards, dangerous chemical mismanagement, or sloppily installed electrical systems that could result in electrocution. What stuck with me as I went on factory "prioritization of issues" audits or reviewed documentary evidence of active governance systems is that regulatory compliance, when properly audited, assessed, and addressed is essential to positive change.

What I discovered after working across these dimensions of system change were two fundamental truths that have guided my work ever since. The first is that business, at scale, has the most significant opportunity to create a thriving planet and a fair society. This in no way diminishes the role that foundations and nonprofits play. What I learned from working with activists and NGOs is how critical their work is within the system. Their expertise in behavior change, cultural narratives, message effectiveness, and a research-based approach to theory of change is essential when it comes to identifying the scope of an issue and the breadth of change needed.

The sheer size and scale of commercial entities drew me back to business as a lever for change. The rise of purpose within the realm of business strategy and a growing realization that a long-term view was better for all stakeholders, including shareholders, had been clearly recognized by more than just me.

When we can organize the entirety of a company's resources to greater good, accomplished within the pursuit of market success, real change can happen. Billion-dollar corporations with millions of customers and tens of thousands of suppliers, with a corporate foundation pouring out resources aligned with their core purpose are a formidable force for good. Especially when collaborating with others like activists and community-based organizations.

Technical change on the ground and the fastidious approach to environmental and worker safety programs that meet regulatory requirements make up the other critical arc in what I was beginning to see as part of the sustainability circle. My years working with environmental scientists, air quality experts, ergonomists, factory safety auditors, and management systems professionals gave me a front-row seat to the massive layer of regulatory frameworks and the experts who manage compliance to worker safety and environmental impact regulation and within rigorous management systems.

Sustainability strategy can be tied to the International Organization for Standardization (ISO)'s systems and certification. ISO is an independent, international NGO with 167 national standards bodies. Through its members, it brings together experts

Table 10.1   How UN SDG sustainability components align with ISO standards

Sustainability Components	ISO Standard
Business Sustainability	ISO 9001 Quality ISO 31000 Risk Management ISO 31010 Risk Assessment
Environmental Sustainability	ISO 14001 Environmental Management
Social Responsibility	ISO 26000 Social Responsibility
Worker Safety	ISO 45001 Occupational Health and Safety

to develop voluntary, consensus-based standards that support innovation and provide a consistent set of solutions to global challenges. When companies adhere to a range of ISO management systems, they have certified outcomes achieved within a globally recognized process for continuous improvement. Additionally, with ISO standards covering almost every subject imaginable, from technical solutions to systems that organize processes and procedures, there are numerous ISO standards that correspond to each of the United Nations' (UN) Sustainable Development Goals (SDG) (Table 10.1).

We absolutely need a compliance framework within which commercial activity is monitored and measured. This need for rigor is already in place within environmental and worker safety realms. And, as we are seeing, it's coming to communications and data transparency too, as we watch the SEC and other global financial institutions codify regulatory requirements for climate and human capital management transparency.

Communications is Key

After years working with community-based organizations and activists, and then pushing for change from the regulatory side, I realized that we cannot achieve systems change without an integrated communication strategy that is embedded from the very beginning of purpose or sustainability strategy. What was missing for me was the dimension of communications as a lever for change within capitalism. Call it sustainability communications or purpose communications, it is an essential element that cannot be overlooked or bolted on later in the change process.

What I know to be true is that moving brands along the purpose journey is really about behavior change—both internally and externally. Once commitments are made and strategies defined, getting buy-in from employees and suppliers will be the most important next step. And then customers, whether those are other businesses or consumers, will need to be brought along because they are an integral part of the value chain of sustainability change. Finally, investors' expectations need to be reset to accommodate a more long-term horizon for returns and a new sense of business value.

A compelling communications strategy is an integral part of purpose change management as it gets operationalized down through sustainability and ESG. This is because, beyond meeting the technical requirements of each of the E, S, and G components, striking the balance required to implement purpose and meet commitments in a way that resonates among multiple stakeholders is hard. For example, when working toward a financial return, the objective is clear: to maximize value for the corporation and its shareholders. But when a company expands its remit to include future generations, it creates a much broader time horizon and the feasible solutions become vastly more complex. Solving for multiple stakeholders is fraught with trade-offs and may even be impossible. This is why a compelling narrative platform and consistent storytelling is so important.

Internally, how does the executive team inspire and reward how managers integrate the incremental ESG dollar as a cost when working toward meeting climate goals? If costs are passed along to customers, how does a brand make the case that true cost accounting is a reasonable tradeoff for lessening climate impact? Or paying livable wages? All these trade-off discussions and decisions must now become part of the ongoing business narrative. Whether included in investor relations, part of reputational management programs and corporate communications, or integrated into marketing claims and packaging copy points, data about what the company is doing operationally and how the product impacts the world are now part of the lexicon.

Understanding the Emotional Dimension

One of my good friends and colleagues, Dr Renee Lertzman, has spent her professional career exploring and understanding an often-overlooked dimension of sustainability communications—the emotional aspect of confronting an existential challenge. Her organization, Project InsideOut is the culmination of studying change agents and how to help them best engage in organizational transformation. While her work at Project InsideOut draws strongly on the best practices in clinical psychological research, it is not just about feelings (Project InsideOut, 2022).

She provides a set of principles that address the complex and messy experiential dimensions of engaging with climate change and how we, as a human society, will transform. Her work explores how cognitive, emotional, and behavioral dimensions must be integrated for effectiveness. Her insights are so important when devising communications as part of sustainability systems change. It is just so different from other business communications. There are dimensions of cognitive dissonance, emotional tumult, and behavioral unknowns that are part of purpose communications. We are in new territory, for sure.

Essentially, what Renee has discovered is that it is essential to meet people where they are, engaging everyone as partners and stakeholders in the work, and bringing a high level of "emotional intelligence" to what we do. Her principles also recognize the highly varied and diverse lived experiences, perspectives, and conditions across human communities and populations. Based on her organization's extensive experience and research, they begin with the assertion that acknowledging and addressing our feelings is a vital and often missing piece of our work.

That is an insight worth repeating. Purposeful brands who want to communicate with all their stakeholders need to begin by creating space to listen to feelings. This is not the customary strategy for communications. Usually, we are trying to grab attention in a cacophony of noise and content. In a way, we are trying to out-shout others, or be more provocative, or persuasive, or clever.

What Renee teaches is that we need to pause and acknowledge all the feelings that could be present when we ask stakeholders to confront climate change or injustice. Existential threats to the future of species or coming face-to-face with human suffering are hard truths to encounter, whether we are talking to investors, employees, or customers.

Taking a high-level look at the five guiding principles from Project InsideOut gives communicators a way to bring emotional intelligence into the planning and deployment of a sustainability strategy and can inform the creation of campaigns, messages, stories, anecdotes, and ongoing implementation.

Principle 1: Attune

Attunement is the building block, key ingredient, capability on which the rest of the Project InsideOut work depends. Attunement is taking the space and time to create mutual understanding on a very deep level. This can happen at the beginning of meetings, with a phrase at the start of a social media post that allows for the acknowledgement of whatever someone might be feeling. With real attunement, we feel it in our bodies and nervous system before we are consciously aware of it. It comes from knowing we are understood, or knowing we are not. This is a practice that goes to the heart of how well we understand our stakeholders and how we demonstrate that understanding.

Attunement is the first step because it is so critical to how we communicate the need for change with our stakeholders. According to Renee, motivation for change only exists in the context of safe and empathetic relationships: within us, with each other, and with our world. She bases this in decades of empirical research into the mechanisms of behavioral change and personal transformation.

Part of attuning includes understanding our own feelings first. Then, we need to create processes that allow us to learn the current set of emotions our stakeholders might be experiencing—anxiety, ambivalence, and aspiration. Often, our own mandates for change, awareness of the stakes, and our own inspirations can blind us to the messy and complicated dilemmas in which others find themselves. So, the creation of skillful survey design, listening circles, focus groups, interviews, ethnography, and social media analysis can be techniques for attuning. The key is to design emotional listening, not just assessing attitudes and beliefs, when we explore our stakeholders' state of mind. We need to know their state of heart too.

Principle 2: Reveal

A challenge in communications is the mistaken notion that we must stay positive, focus on success, hide our fears and failures to keep people engaged. But what Renee has learned in her research is that revealing the hard feelings is key to authentic engagement and yields better outcomes. For brands, this means being open and honest about challenges and barriers to meeting climate commitments or addressing complex equity issues. In developing messages, campaigns, and ongoing updates, it is important to include the tough and difficult aspects and not just the wins. Doing so makes it safer for others to face and move through their challenges—and this is a key to sustaining engagement from stakeholders, especially employees.

A tricky part of revealing the tough challenges or the ways in which obstacles have arisen is to create "hero" narratives that show the challenges and then how they were overcome. This is just another version of the positivity trap—we don't always have a brilliant solution or a tenaciously successful outcome. Sometimes we hit a roadblock and must take a pause, or completely redirect. This type of honest communication builds trust and empathy.

It is also important not to oversimplify, sugarcoat, or greenwash either the challenge or the efforts taken to meet commitments. This is true for external communications as well as team meetings. As leaders, we can consistently model how to acknowledge challenging feelings and mistakes, giving others the space to do so as well.

Principle 3: Convene

True convening within a communications program means creating space for diverse voices, lived experiences and opinions in your campaign. It goes beyond identifying groups and then directing unilateral messages at them. To allow for a real sense of belonging, and to create agency among those you are rallying for change, it requires feedback loops, intake systems, and means for contributing. Create internal events that include panels and experts and allow adequate time for discussion following the presentation of information, commitments, and metrics. Allow time for breakouts and the integration of a mix of voices and opinions.

It can seem counterintuitive in a time of great urgency to create the time and space needed for quality participation, getting everyone's voice in the mix, and leveraging the power of small groups and pairs. But the investment in true convening creates a sense of agency and participation that will be needed to undertake the hard work of carbon reduction or meeting diversity goals. Stakeholder communications requires that we gather audiences, users, participants, communities, lists, followers, and enable them to work with each other. This means we are more of a convener, less of a mobilizer.

Principle 4: Equip

As the people responsible for driving purpose across an organization, and getting all stakeholders to understand and participate in driving to environmental and social commitments, we are usually the subject matter experts. Creating capacity across our stakeholder groups is key to long-term change and maintaining the momentum needed to withstand setbacks or inertia. People are hungry for tools and resources for supporting resilience.

I have seen this in many instances when working with brands who are deploying an internal communications program around climate commitments. Once the overall goal has been established, there are a wide range of activities that individuals can take to help drive down emissions. Some people will want to dig into the specifics, understand the science, and create solutions that go beyond initial requirements. These individuals need a resource center that has all the background information, recommended reading lists, podcasts, interviews, and other experts.

Whether motivated by curiosity or diverse learning styles, equipping employees with a robust resource center allows each to advance at their own pace. Organizational change management depends on capacity building. When you provide people control over something they care about, they increase their investment as well as their abilities. When you build capabilities, enable people to run with their work, you amplify their contributions and give them more autonomy.

Principle 5: Sustain

Maintaining enthusiasm and engagement over the long term is a critical component in communicating purpose or sustainability initiatives. Whether launching employee communication campaigns or hosting big external commitment events during global moments like Earth Day or Climate Week, the flurry and excitement will wane over time. When designing campaigns and change management programs, an important element is the long-term component. This can include planned and periodic updates that feature examples, case studies or anecdotes demonstrating how something has been accomplished and who helped create the progress. Build in structures that track and celebrate people's actions and engagement, like story-banking sites or other places where people can upload examples. For example, if your company uses Slack for peer-to-peer communications, you can create a channel for employees to post their community volunteer activities like working in their child's classroom, participating in a beach cleanup, or working the polls on election day. Ask them to post a photo and a caption. As the internal communications team monitors the channel, they can quickly find the stories and employees who could be featured in the annual report or in an internal webinar. Teach people to run these and know they have a community of practice from which to get input, support, and learning.

When practiced together, these five principles make each of us an effective and empathetic guide. According to Renee:

> To face our current realities, and stay engaged, awake, and capable, we need to do more than scare, inform or push solutions at people. Our work must be more nuanced. It starts with our capacity to show up as fully human. When we start with ourselves—and our own messy and complicated feelings—we can begin conversations that transform.
>
> (Project InsideOut, 2022).

Communications for Good

In Chapter 8 we explored how to develop a purpose platform and create a sustainability narrative platform under which all the commitments, strategies and programs can be organized into pillars. In addition to a clear narrative platform, key messages, and strong narrative elements, communicating about sustainability initiatives requires ongoing, consistent, and creative content deployed across owned, earned, and paid channels.

There are three categories of content that need to be collected and distributed through a range of devices (long form copy, infographics, videos, speeches, panels, events, celebrations) to audiences whose information needs will vary and change over time. Audiences include employees and recruits, customers, suppliers and partners, investors, policy makers and regulators, and the communities where the business has a presence—whether those are stores, offices, manufacturing, data centers, warehouses, or distribution centers.

Each audience will need some combination and range of detail across three content groups: vision, data, and stories. Brand vision is a critical component of effective communication because it sets the context and gives stakeholders a sense of the long-term outcomes for which the brand is willing to take responsibility. Purpose statements, coupled with sustainability strategy and corporate values, are the components of vision content. These need to be connected to the brand, be aspirational and compelling. They should describe the prospective state that the company is working toward and how its innovation and commitments will help deliver a better future.

Internal Communications

A strong internal communications program that supports operationalizing of sustainability goals is the best means to help people know both what to do and how to do it to be successful. It helps define what success looks like at both the collective, organization level and how employee actions help them meet individual key performance indicators.

In many ways, this internal communications process mimics those deployed in enterprise-wide changes like quality—remember Six Sigma? Or like creating a culture of safety. What happens is that a new way of working is now expected of employees. Deploying environmental and social benefits as new decision filters for every business decision requires inspiration, information, activation, and ongoing transformation. These four phases of an internal communications campaign have specific elements that will help reach employees.

Before we look at the four phases, it is important to think about employees not as a monolithic group but rather as a blend of colleagues who will have a range of responsibility for delivering on climate and DEI goals, depending upon where they sit in the organization. Segmentation of the employee base is a critical first step.

First, classification into desked and undesked employees is important when developing an internal communications program. Many times, desked employees work in more centralized departments—but not always. They tend to be in more office-like settings or are mostly remote workers who spend all day in front of the computer screen in their homes. Thinking about how to inspire and motivate these employees will look different than those who are undesked.

Employees who do not spend almost all their time in front of computer screens are, instead, driving trucks and vehicles, using handheld devices for information intake, moving objects in and out of distribution centers, managing or participating in manufacturing processes or assembly of products. They can also be deployed into patient or customer homes, or work in retail locations across urban, rural, or suburban locations.

The messages and means for reaching this wide range of what is arguably the most important stakeholder in change management will need to be carefully developed and deployed.

Beyond where and how people work, there is also a range of departments and business functions that will require a more direct integration with the sustainability commitments while others will be integrated later in the process. I believe it is a mistake to assume that only leaders or managers have the responsibility for, or opportunity even, to drive real and meaningful change within a company.

There's a story I heard back in 2008, which had become part of the Walmart sustainability journey lore, that I have often wondered about. Some digging took me to the company's 2015 *Walmart World* employee magazine to find out about Darrell Meyer and confirm that what I heard was true (Walmart, 2015). As a part of the company's 2007 Personal Sustainability Projects program, then assistant manager Darrell Myers presented an idea to take the light bulbs out of the vending machines in the back rooms of the store. Since they burned 24 hours a day, 365 days a year, it was estimated that they were costing $102 per year, per machine, on energy costs. By simply removing the lightbulb in every drink machine in every employee break room, it was estimated that Walmart saved close to $1 million in energy costs that year (Jones, 2007).

This story has stuck with me because it always reminds me that you never know where a good idea will come from. Job titles, roles, and even explicitly stated responsibilities are not always the best predictors of where success in innovating for positive impact will come from.

However, even given the belief that creativity and innovation can come from anyone, there is in fact a disciplined method for cascading strategy and change requirements to those most affected first, even as you take the time to provide top line information and inspiration to everyone. Generally, those who should be in the first wave of information are those closest to the material changes that need to be made. These "critical path" employees need the most detailed information, should have access to resources and a change team for support, and be given specific channels of communication for feedback loops and the collection of anecdotal success and failure stories.

For example, if a social sustainability goal of increasing diverse representation in leadership has become the most important target for the next three years, then recruiters and executive leadership are the initial stakeholder group for change management communications. They will be most directly involved in recruiting and promoting candidates for consideration. Certainly, every employee can learn about the initiative and take pride when progress is made. But the most affected group that must change their behaviors and drive change are the hiring managers and executives who are the most directly responsible for ensuring a diverse leadership team.

When deploying a comprehensive internal communications program for engaging all employees in the purpose commitments and sustainability goals, these four distinct phases are designed to target both critical path employees and the rest of the workforce.

Before the official launch of your brand purpose or sustainability platform, it is important to gain internal alignment across the leadership team that will be responsible for driving change. They will be key players to further communicate the messages behind your purpose or sustainability goals and you will need them to link their strategies more clearly to it. During a leader briefing, you will want to cover how the newly articulated purpose is central to the business and the journey behind how it was defined. Some of these key players likely helped shape it, but everyone will need to be brought along and understand the process, who was involved and how further refinements will be integrated over time.

Secondly, your key players are your purpose champions, and a prelaunch briefing is the place to set expectations for how you expect them to bring this work to their teams and into their part of the business. It will not be possible to have every dimension of this worked at, because you will want each leader to bring their unique perspective and talents to how purpose gets operationalized or how environmental and social commitments are met. However, clear expectations that these dimensions are now a new way of doing business will need to be clearly set.

Next is to share what is coming next from a launch perspective and the road map from communicating to all employees. Lastly, be ready to share what resources will be made available to them to bring this work to their teams so that they can have the needed discussions with their teams, clarify questions or uncertainties, and refine the action plans that will bring commitments and impacts to life

Phase 1: Inspiration

Once key leaders have been pre-briefed, you can move to the launch. This first phase is all about generating enthusiasm from the entire workforce but then moving them quickly to action. This launch phase is an important milestone moment that officially marks the beginning of a collective journey and formally invites everyone to engage, follow, celebrate, and contribute. As we explored in the Project InsideOut section previously, sustaining momentum beyond the launch phase is important. But don't underestimate the power of a beginning moment. This is the time for a rousing manifesto video, inspiring words from leaders, examples of what's been tested throughout the organization or early progress on ESG programs. There can be examples of what brands have done or descriptions of what the journey is going to look like.

Other elements of the launch can include social and intranet content and the debut of a central resource center so that interested employees can learn at their own pace and dig deep into topics that might interest them. One of the best ways to kick off purpose and sustainability is a Town Hall event—with live or pre-recorded content. A range of other materials and launch items can include new brand guidelines or graphic elements like email signatures, signage, Slack messages, zoom backgrounds, and even shirts or other "swag."

One thing to consider is useful and durable items for employees or even a range of options they can order to avoid the negative environmental impact of corporate items that never really get used.

Phase 2: Information

The second phase is not just a moment in time, but has a timeframe designed to distribute as much information as needed to make the vision and commitment real across the organization. Whether this phase is a couple of weeks, or several months, the idea is to dimensionalize the commitments and near-term milestones across functions and within each product or brand organization so that every employee has at least a high-level understanding of what is now "business as usual."

Coupled with the road show, it is recommended that listening sessions are also included. This will be the first chance to hear from a wide range of employees (both desked and undesked), in a multitude of regions, to gauge areas of confusion and enthusiasm, and identify potential on-the-ground champions who can help advance the initiatives. One element of the road show that has proven to be successful is showcasing speakers, using videos, or having the individuals Zoom in to local meetings, with their personal stories of actions they've taken. In every case where I have helped companies deploy a communications campaign, whether internal or external, there are always anecdotal stories of people or teams that have been working on environmental or social impact projects in an ad hoc way. These become early fodder for storytelling and help others see themselves. Too often, climate commitments or DEI strategies can come across as theoretical or high level, and the average worker wonders how this is relevant to their individual job function. Examples of the changes people have made in their processes or habits is a great way to bring commitments and progress to life.

Phase 3: Activation

The third phase is the most detailed and comprehensive and is designed to move into tangible operationalizing of sustainability commitments into business behaviors. This phase is a direct call to action across all critical path departments. One of the most important elements of this phase will be structured discussions to identify the necessary actions that will impact goals and along what cadence and timeline. This can take place in workshops with functional leaders to ideate around actions, metrics, timelines, and milestones.

For example, in programs aimed at reducing packaging, this would involve workshops with departments such as procurement, R&D, manufacturing, and brand to explore all of the cascading dimensions when considering replacing one packaging material (petroleum plastic) with another (paper or bio plastic). There will be sourcing, price, manufacturing process, and timing considerations that will all need to be discussed, explored, and weighed. The outcomes of these early workshops become informative for setting KPIs and other milestones as well as early formation of the storytelling around successes and barriers encountered. These sessions are important for further rolling out of goals and milestones to set the pace of change.

Phase 4: Transformation

Think of this phase as the steady drumbeat of internal communications that will now become part of all other messages aimed at the workforce. Alongside missives about benefits, compulsory trainings, or cybersecurity requirements, sustainability program updates and instructions become a way for employees to participate in continuous improvement. Demonstrate ongoing climate progress with data visualization that appears in gathering places or on internal Slack channels or Teams sites. Another way to normalize ESG progress is to consider recognition by integrating with existing awards and review programs.

The storytelling component will be important and can feature ongoing employee, department, or brand spotlights that showcase those that are doing this work well. The key is to reveal, over time, the ways in which the company is becoming transformed and has integrated its purpose into the business itself. This phase brings everyone along on the sustainability journey, engendering pride at both the individual and organizational level.

The internal communications program is just one component. Integrating a robust external communications strategy and program is another important way to ensure all key stakeholders are part of the systems change.

External Communications

A successful external communications program is one that builds on the internal communications program, designed to showcase how a company's transformation to becoming a purposeful brand and bring all its external stakeholders along. In the same way that you need all employees to understand their role in contributing to a thriving planet and an equitable society through the business itself, you also need all other stakeholders engaged in the same effort. Lastly, brands who are making progress can help accelerate their work by talking explicitly about successes and failures, giving other companies permission and the knowledge needed to move forward as well.

A term I call "green hushing" is as damaging to purposeful brands as greenwashing. Not getting credit for the work you do affects brand value and reputation. It also slows down collective progress. Over the many years I have been doing this work, we always begin with a landscape scan—what are competitors doing? What are others doing? Where is the innovation? What is best practice? Studying the landscape helps leapfrog innovation and spurs progress in tackling the urgent issues of our times.

Messages

Sharp, concise, and inspirational messages are the backbone of an external communications program. These are built from the sustainability/ESG platform developed at the beginning of the operational process. However, these need to be refined and tested for each audience segment, including the various proof points that support and bring to life each pillar. From there, create a message guide and supporting storylines, and identify the executives who will be the primary spokespersons for each dimension or pillar in the program.

Another often overlooked dimension of the communications strategy is the inclusion of purpose messages into all existing corporate efforts. From the website to email signatures, from the 10-K annual report to investor briefings, across sales materials and even on packaging or instore, as the purpose becomes integral to strategy it naturally belongs as part of the ongoing corporate narrative.

Yearlong Specific Sustainability Program

Once a brand has a clear purpose and the sustainability strategy that will operationalize it, this integrated intention to do business better deserves its own holistic communications program. One that continuously reports on ongoing sustainability and ESG commitments and initiatives, and the success and challenges met in delivering against vision and goals.

A comprehensive plan should include storyline and media pitching recommendations targeting across business, consumer, and sustainability media. A good cadence can also include three to five "tentpole" moments for communications, like program launches, commitment announcements or major goal achievements. The program can also include efforts tied to affinity moments like Earth Day, World Environment Day, Black History Month, or the anniversary of the company's commitments.

It is also good to look for opportunities to showcase progress and calls-to-action at conferences, panels, or on LinkedIn that can also be leveraged for placement on owned social media platforms and within other awareness-building efforts. Paid content series that feature bylines from key executives are a good way for companies to share detailed content that helps explain the intricacies of a particular effort—like migrating from fossil fuels to renewable energy sources or the complexities of identifying and solving pay equity gaps. Another element worth exploring that can help communicate program progress and address challenges is to convene salon-style stakeholder and influencer discussions at existing industry events or trade association meetings to reach smaller groups of critical external stakeholders.

Leveraging Conversations

Opportunistic communications is one of the best ways to participate in the cultural conversations that have the most saliency for the purposeful brand. By identifying keywords and topics to monitor, a brand can illuminate the influencers and platforms that are exploring solutions aligned with theirs and look for authentic and relevant ways to participate.

It is important to take a pause and remember the risk of performative communications efforts in the public sphere. It is a careful course for a brand to navigate. Even as there are media conversations and trending topics that seem relevant for spokespeople to comment on, the key is to have a clear position, tangible proof points, and a humble attitude.

The most important dimension of purpose or sustainability communication is that it is enduring and integrated. Whether the purpose story shows up in reputation management efforts, corporate communications platforms, marketing campaigns, sales materials, or social media feeds, it is now an integral part of the brand story and should be showcased regularly.

References

Jones, T (2007) Wal-Mart associate sees the light, *Greensboro News & Record*

Project InsideOut (2022) A new world is emerging, Project InsideOut, https://projectinsideout.net (archived at https://perma.cc/2V3M-9RFF)

Walmart (2015) Moments. People. Celebration, *Walmart World*, https://one.walmart.com/content/dam/us-wire-wm1/images/company/news/walmart_world/magazine/pdf/2015/2015july.pdf (archived at https://perma.cc/8SAF-4HNZ)

Conclusion: What's Next?

When it Comes to Our Future, Hope is a Choice

I used to see myself as an optimist. Occasionally I received the critique that I was a Pollyanna or wore rose-colored glasses too often. What I have come to understand about myself over the years, is that I am a practical idealist, maintaining a vision for a better world while simultaneously holding the truth of systemic challenges.

The state of the world today is sobering. There are more extreme weather events, caused by too much carbon in the atmosphere, that are creating an environmental diaspora that is only beginning to expand. We are watching strident isolationist and anti-refugee sentiments surface again—as it has time and time again throughout human history—just as those displaced by disasters and dictators are on the move in growing numbers. We are watching supply chains falter and readily available resources dwindle. More viruses are emerging and social inequities threaten to keep the vulnerable and marginalized in harm's way. The pandemic exposed our society's more serious cracks and also revealed the best of human nature.

These are not times for the faint-hearted. But they are for the whole-hearted. For the system-thinker. For the practical idealist and the hopeful. I agree with the words of author Rebecca Traister:

> [W]hile it is incumbent on us to digest the scope and breadth of the badness, it is equally our responsibility not to despair... we go forward with the will of those who came before, and those who have never stopped putting one foot in front of another, to some finer tomorrow, distant but always possible.
>
> (Traister, 2022)

There are signs of hope, and reasons to believe that all of us are working to meet this moment. Racism, sexism, and injustice are being called out in real time, even in the face of push-back and dismissal from decades-hardened white supremacists and misogynists. The cost of renewables is below fossil fuels for the first time and funding for climate innovation and infrastructure improvements is flowing. Activists continue to call for attention and action—on worker conditions, the climate, political systems, voter access.

Businesses are operating within this growing complexity and grappling with the reality of shared value, shared risk. The veneer of separateness, that any business can succeed in isolation from responsibility for social systems or environmental resources, is eroding.

From my perspective, I am seeing two types of business responses. For those who have a clear understanding of the greater good they are creating in the world by embracing and operationalizing purpose, they are still innovating. Specifically, they are experimenting with enterprise-wide change management and working to bring an environmental and social filter to every business decision, to every dimension. Their ambition is to create an entire value chain, from suppliers to customers, into a community of stakeholders all contributing to a better world through commerce.

They are also innovating around products—engaging with consumers to find the right mix of quality, price, environmental impact, and consumer action that will drive growth and loyalty. Fashion brands experimenting with refurbished clothing lines, like Kirrin Finch in Brooklyn, New York whose Pre-Loved line supports peer-to-peer selling as well as selling factory samples of the company's popular androgynous suits and shirts (Kirrin Finch, 2022). There are a number of consumer-packaged goods companies collaborating with retailers and reclamation companies like Loop to provide a steady stream of refillable shampoo, orange juice, deodorant, and ice cream containers so that consumers can subscribe to the contents and the manufacturers maintain responsibility for the packaging. Just like the old days of the milkman delivering bottles of milk to American households every morning in the 1940s and 1950s.

The second type of business response is coming from those new to defining their purpose or deploying a comprehensive sustainability strategy. These companies, while predominantly B2B, have assumed that purpose and sustainability were relevant to other brands but not to themselves. Many B2B companies felt that purpose, showing up on social issues, or delivering environmentally friendly products were the purview of brands who have consumers to please. For the last two decades, these companies were complying with EPA regulations or meeting Occupational Safety and Health Administration (OSHA) requirements for worker safety, but had not seen purpose and sustainability as a driver for value and innovation.

Regardless of where a company is on their purpose journey, to ensure progress and relevance for the next 50 years I think there are a few guidelines that will work. To begin, is humanity at the core and are basic human values central to purpose? This is where every company needs to ensure dignity, justice, equity, and inclusion are built into the heart of the business. Success will come because of purpose, not in spite of it. This takes courage to push for more, to do better, reach higher, and center business progress alongside what the world needs—a fair society and a thriving planet. We all need to be willing to step up our commitments to protecting and nurturing the commons. Our young people are pushing all of us to stop wasting time, stop focusing on things that don't really matter when it comes to wellbeing and happiness. We need them as we look ahead and they should be empowered and included as we build purposeful brands.

So where is purpose headed in the next decade? What do those who are hard at work as chief sustainability officers and change agents believe that the future holds? I reached out to a handful of my colleagues with a simple prompt: What does the next decade hold for purpose, sustainability, and brands?

> **Purpose as vision:** More than the raison d'être for an organization, purpose as strategy will serve as a valuable frame to guide an enterprise and its leaders, and inform choices and trade-offs related to business decisions and capital allocations required to meet the opportunities and challenges of the future. Purpose-led brands will create authentic, culturally relevant, trusted connections with consumers, which can

inspire measurable actions to create a more diverse, equitable, inclusive and sustainable future for all. At Mattel, our purpose is to empower the next generation to explore the wonder of childhood and reach their full potential. Purpose has been the north star guiding our company transformation and will light our way going forward.

(Pamela Gill-Alabaster, SVP, Global Sustainability and
Social Impact, Mattel, Inc)

Purpose as a dose of reality: With early leaders having committed, tested, learned, failed, and realized just how difficult sustainability is— especially in shifting consumption and consumer behavior change—we are at a crossroad. We can either take the red pill and acknowledge the truth of what people and planet are facing and keep after it, or we take the blue pill denying what lies ahead, wait and see, delay pilots, delay collaboration, and run greater risk in the out-years as many of our mid- and long-term commitments come to term. I'd rather keep after it, knowing breakthrough could be just around the corner.

(Paula Alexander, Director of Sustainability and Responsible
Sourcing, Burt's Bees)

Purpose norms and surprises: I believe sustainability in companies is only getting more embedded and the table stakes are rising. A few megatrends in particular are driving this—transparency and generational norms shifting, i.e., younger generations expect more of business. That shift in norms is what I'm most hopeful about. Those are deep changes that are impossible to avoid. There is obviously lots to be worried about—misinformation and attacks on truth are dangerous, and the decline of democracy and rise of fascism is a big headwind to do the kind of collective work that our biggest problems require. And surprises? I'm sure we will be surprised by what issues grab people's attention. Plastics and packaging took a big leap forward because one turtle had a straw up its nose.

(Andrew Winston, Author, Net Positive)

Purpose as innovation: After 20 years of watching this space, I can truly say the bar has been raised, and I am increasingly hopeful that the future will go to those brands that excel at and compete around innovation for environmental and social benefit. Of course, the risk is that we have another setback due to new players coming on to the scene making unsubstantiated claims, either intentionally, or unintentionally, and in so doing dealing a blow to consumer trust. However, what gives me most hope is the depth of understanding now present among those multinationals we have been dealing with for close to two decades now. While the need is more pressing, so is our knowledge base, as well as the sophistication of the tools and solutions providers coming into the mix.

I'm especially excited about the burgeoning bio-materials innovation space, and the use of AI and machine learning to accelerate the process of designing solutions that are environmentally benign, and serve to either reduce the output of carbon or sequester carbon as a "designed-in" part of their performance criteria and properties. Furthermore, I see more and more systems thinking taking place, not only within business, but among consumers who are asking more questions about the broader impacts of the purchases they are making. Working together, especially under a coordinated effort by brands to leverage their influence across the economic ecosystem, we can have real hope of shifting to the sustainably regenerative economy of the future.

(KoAnn Vikoren Skrzyniarz, Founder/CEO, Sustainable Brands)

Purpose in marketing: I am encouraged that our conversation in marketing has advanced from "Should my brand be talking about purpose and sustainability?" to "How can my brand engage consumers in its journey towards creating a more sustainable and just world in a way that drives growth for the business?" The conversation is also now shifting from "With sustainability, we sacrifice short term sales for long term brand building" to "We can and must do both to ensure the business and our society thrives." In the next decade I expect more employers to seek talent that excels in purpose driven marketing.

(Maddy Kulkarni, Global Marketing Director,
Sustainability and Social Impact, PepsiCo)

Purpose becomes strategy: In the next decade, I think we will see the emergence of two categories of brands—the ones that do their best to do less harm and those who thrive by doing more good. Regardless of if brands are harm reducers or positive impactors, there will no longer be any leeway given to brands that simply make pledges not connected to tangible action and progress. I also believe that we will see purpose completely integrated into business strategy to the point that "purposeful brands" will be a pleonasm. Just like there used to be digital marketing plans, there are now just marketing plans that include digital. This will happen to purpose strategy; it will simply become business strategy with purpose deeply embedded into every dimension.

(Virginie Helias, Chief Sustainability Officer, Procter & Gamble)

In Summary—Live a Life on Purpose

The best gift I experience from the work I do is the beauty of a congruent life. It's not perfect, but for more than 30 years, the last 15 especially, my work and career have been aligned with my sense of personal purpose and allow me to work every day in addressing the need for an equitable society and a thriving planet. I hope this book has given you some practical tips and techniques for implementing purpose at your workplace as well as a sense of community with all of us who are on that same journey. I like to keep these five ideas in mind as I make choices for myself, my family, my colleagues and my work:

Live "Yes—and."

Build something.

Bring others.

Nurture the commons.

Find beauty.

References

Kirrin Finch (2022) Preloved, Kirrin Finch, https://kirrinfinch.treet.co/about/info (archived at https://perma.cc/BKB5-8APU)

Traister, R (2022) The necessity of hope in post-Roe America, The Cut, www.thecut.com/2022/06/rebecca-traister-on-the-necessity-of-hope.html (archived at https://perma.cc/Z6XN-LFCL)

INDEX